52-Week Basketball Training

Chip Sigmon

Human Kinetics

Library of Congress Cataloging-in-Publication Data

Sigmon, Chip, 1955-
    52-week basketball training / Chip Sigmon.
        p. cm
Includes bibliographical references (p.   ).
    ISBM 0-7360-4514-7 (Soft cover)
    1. Basketball--Training. 2. Basketball--Coaching. I. Title:
Fifty-two week basketball training. II. Title.
    GV885.35.S54 2003
    796.323.'07--dc21

                                        2003005361

ISBN-10: 0-7360-4514-7
ISBN-13: 978-0-7360-4514-8

Copyright © 2003 by Chip Sigmon

The Web addresses cited in this text were current as of June 1, 2003, unless otherwise noted.

Acquisitions Editor: Edward McNeely; **Developmental Editor:** Julie Rhoda; **Assistant Editor:** Carla Zych; **Copyeditor:** Patsy Fortney; **Proofreader:** Julie Marx Goodreau; **Graphic Designer:** Nancy Rasmus; **Graphic Artist:** Francine Hamerski; **Photo and Art Manager:** Dan Wendt; **Cover Designer:** Jack W. Davis; **Photographer (cover):** © Nathaniel S. Butler/Getty Images; **Photographer (interior):** all photos by Garrett Ellwood unless otherwise noted; **Illustrator:** Mic Greenberg; **Printer:** Versa Press

Human Kinetics books are available at special discounts for bulk purchase. Special editions or book excerpts can also be created to specification. For details, contact the Special Sales Manager at Human Kinetics.

Printed in the United States of America   10 9 8 7 6 5 4 3

Human Kinetics
Web site: www.HumanKinetics.com

United States: Human Kinetics
P.O. Box 5076
Champaign, IL 61825-5076
800-747-4457
e-mail: humank@hkusa.com

Canada: Human Kinetics
475 Devonshire Road Unit 100
Windsor, ON N8Y 2L5
800-465-7301 (in Canada only)
e-mail: orders@hkcanada.com

Europe: Human Kinetics
107 Bradford Road
Stanningley
Leeds LS28 6AT, United Kingdom
+44 (0) 113 255 5665
e-mail: hk@hkeurope.com

Australia: Human Kinetics
57A Price Avenue
Lower Mitcham, South Australia 5062
08 8372 0999
e-mail: liaw@hkaustralia.com

New Zealand: Human Kinetics
Division of Sports Distributors NZ Ltd.
P.O. Box 300 226 Albany
North Shore City
Auckland
0064 9 448 1207
e-mail: info@humankinetics.co.nz

To my beautiful wife, Michelle, for her love and support and for helping me become a better person and father. To my daughters, Sinclaire and Sydney: These two have changed my life for the best. Also to my mom and dad, whom I love so!

Strength and conditioning have been a part of my life, but these people have always been my life.

I thank God for the wisdom and discipline to complete the task and always finish strong.

Contents

Foreword

The game of basketball has changed dramatically over the years for both men and women. Players are stronger and faster and can jump higher than ever before. It used to be that a player started to prepare for the upcoming season maybe four to six weeks before the start of training camp or the first day of practice. Now athletes have to take care of themselves year-round. If players at any level of the sport want to improve their game from year to year, they must commit themselves to a full-year training program that is structured, challenging, and productive.

Therefore, coaching in this day and age can be rewarding yet challenging. As a coach, you've got to know what buttons to push to make the player respond. But it's much easier to coach and direct a player or team that is in top-notch condition. It's great when the basketball coach can focus on the Xs and Os of the game instead of worrying about a player's physical conditioning. A player who is not in top physical condition at the beginning of the season will always be a step slower when it comes to performance and will likely be more susceptible to injury.

Because of our experience playing and coaching, we know what it takes to reach goals, and we understand the dedication it takes to improve in all areas of your game. There are no shortcuts; you simply must make a commitment to get to the level you want to reach!

We both have seen athletes with a great deal of talent but very little work ethic. We have also seen athletes with limited talent whose tremendous work ethic helped elevate them to the top and who were able to compete at a high performance and skill level.

If you have that burning desire to be at your very best during game time, then Chip's *52-Week Basketball Training* will keep you headed in the right direction. In today's world of complex training programs, Chip keeps it simple and easy to follow; yet he will challenge you to reach the top. Chip covers every area of the game when it comes to basketball conditioning. From agility, balance, and explosive strength work to specific basketball conditioning drills, you'll find it here in the program presented in this book.

We have had the privilege of working with Chip, and we know you'll find these workouts and programs a key resource in your basketball preparation that will lead you to success. Go have fun, work hard, and become the best that you can be!

Paul Silas, Head Coach, Cleveland Cavaliers (NBA)
Anne Donovan, Head Coach, Seattle Storm (WNBA)

Introduction

The first principle on which the game of basketball was based was that it should demand of, and develop in, the player the highest type of physical and athletic development.—**Dr. James Naismith, May 1914**

Not too many years ago basketball players were discouraged from weight training or any sport-specific drills pertaining to resistance work. Experts once thought that these activities were detrimental to the athlete. We now understand the importance of weight training, conditioning, and specialized drills and their role in the advancement of the game of basketball. I have been fortunate to work on all levels of athletics from elementary school to middle school, high school, college, and the professional level. I have seen the direct benefits that athletes achieve through sport-specific strength and conditioning programs.

In the NBA, for example, basketball is a different game than it was 10 or 15 years ago. Even on the college level the game has become more physical. Players are stronger, quicker, and more explosive. Why? Because players know how beneficial physical conditioning is for basketball, how it improves their game, even how it makes them feel—just ask any of them!

These same players train year-round, from off-season to preseason and even during the season. Because of this emphasis on year-round training, every team in the NBA, WNBA, NFL, NHL, Major League Baseball, and most colleges, big or small, have someone to oversee the strength and conditioning program. This is evidence of just how far the physical aspect of the game of basketball has come and the benefits that can be achieved from having a specific strengthening and conditioning program.

No matter what your age, gender, or skill level, *52-Week Basketball Training* shows you how to achieve your goals through physical conditioning. It guides you year-round in the right direction with your training program and takes all the guesswork out of your formula for success. Using the program presented here, you'll know what to do each week and how to do it.

The workouts described in this 52-week training program are divided into four seasons—off-season, preseason, in-season, and postseason. Each training season workout offers you the opportunity to achieve optimum conditioning and performance for that particular season.

This book gives you direction in your training, but you need to start with your own unique goals to give this training a purpose. Delineating your goals helps you become the best basketball player you can be. Before starting your off-season training program, I strongly recommend that you take some time to write down your goals and date them so you can look back and see how you are progressing.

Be specific about what you want to accomplish with your basketball-specific skills as well as your strength, speed, and conditioning improvements.

Part I of this book details how to prepare for conditioning and provides your specific week-by-week workouts. Part II then provides the descriptions and illustrations of the specific exercises and drills that are included in each workout.

Chapter 1 explains the conditioning tests the NBA and WNBA strength and conditioning coaches give to their players. This chapter also offers specific tests you can take to give you a performance baseline of where you are and help you decide where you want to go. Take these tests during the first and last weeks of the off-season phase, and again in the last week of the preseason phase.

The off-season training is divided into three phases, as described in chapter 2. The first phase centers on building basic strength. Basketball is a game of explosive movements, both lateral and horizontal. To be explosive or to improve your explosiveness, you must start with a good strength base. This is the cornerstone of your year-round training program. During the first phase you prepare your body for sport-specific movements using basic resistance exercises. Along with basic strength building in phase I, you start your overall conditioning by establishing a good aerobic base.

After preparing your body with basic strength movements from phase I of the off-season, you are ready for phases II and III, which introduce some sport-specific exercises to improve your explosiveness, quickness, and speed. Your conditioning at this point takes you to the running track and baseball field for some middle-distance running work that will enhance the short sprints you start to do in the next season—the preseason.

Now it's time to put your training into high gear! You've got six weeks of preseason training and two weeks of training camp (see chapter 3) until the in-season. Typically during this preseason time players are hitting the court every day playing one-on-one or pickup games. One-on-one games can be played half court, but pickup games should be full court if at all possible to help with the conditioning process.

In the weight room during the preseason phase you combine resistance work, conditioning, and balance and quickness drills all in the same workout. At this point you are right in the middle of sport-specific training for basketball. You move from one exercise to the other with little rest to improve your muscular endurance, and you are called on to be quick and explosive even when tired from the preceding exercises. That's what the game of basketball is all about—getting that rebound after the third or even the fourth try, then sprinting down the court and rotating and cutting to come off the screen or to set the screen.

I call the last two weeks of the preseason phase training camp. This is the time to focus your attention on getting ready for the first game. All the weeks of off-season and preseason work and dedication come into play at this time. Because you need all of your energy for the demands of basketball-specific practice, you take out all resistance work during the first week of training camp. Some coaches may even have practices twice a day, so you'll need valuable rest time. You'll then start back on weight training the second week, working the major muscle groups only.

Your conditioning during these two weeks of training camp is an important part of practice as you put the finishing touches on what you have been working on so hard during the off-season and preseason phases. Your conditioning from this point until the end of the season is primarily short sprint and agility (moving in different directions quickly) work.

Once your regular season games start, your in-season training consists of resistance work and conditioning work twice a week (see chapter 4). Depending on your schedule, you may be doing some resistance work the day before a game. This should in no way hinder your play because of the lighter percentages of weights you are lifting during this time. I have had players do a short, light, 20- to 30-minute weight training program on game day with tremendous results. I discuss this more in chapter 4.

When two teams are equally matched, the better-conditioned team always wins out. That is why keeping your body in top physical condition even during the season is so critical. Your conditioning sessions can be conducted before or after practice (depending on your coach's decision). Conditioning sessions at the beginning of practice are sometimes good because players have to learn to play at their best when they are tired. Conditioning sessions should also be short but intense. This is one of the ways to keep an individual or team from burning out during a long season. A variety of conditioning drills should be planned and available during this time to ensure top conditioning levels.

After the season, the tournaments, and the championship games are over, your postseason training will be a time to refresh and reflect (see chapter 5). Your body needs rest for a while after the season. Your joints may be sore and need time to heal. Your "active rest" is important also and is discussed in more detail in chapter 5. This is a time when your body becomes active again while mentally you are away from the pressures of the game.

You also need to reflect on the past season and write down the highs and lows and what you learned from both. During this active rest your body grows hungry again to train, to get better, to fall in love with accomplishments, and to see the results of physical conditioning.

Chapter 6 gives you an overview of flexibility training as well as 20 stretches that you can include in your conditioning to improve your flexibility. Chapter 7 provides descriptions of the strength and power exercises while chapters 8 and 9 describe drills to hone your speed, basketball-specific quickness and agility, and ball handling.

What are you waiting for? Let's go train!

Acknowledgments

A special thanks to Kirsten Ranells for her typing and editing; Adrienne Garabedian, secretary for the Charlotte Hornets; Dr. Ken Jones, former strength and conditioning coach for Gardner Webb University; and Jonathan Supranowitz, assistant media relations director for the New York Knicks.

A special thanks also to Alex McKechnie for teaching me what *core* training really is, and to Garrett Ellwood for the great pictures.

I would like to thank Jim Morris, former baseball coach and now professor at Appalachian State University for helping me get started in the strength and conditioning field. I would also like to thank Dr. Mike Stone, Dr. Howard O'Bryant, and Dr. Vaughn Christian for their wisdom and guidance over many years.

Exercise and Drill Finder

Exercise or drill name	Workout phase				Page # of exercise description
	Off-season Wk 1-21	Preseason Wk 22-29	In-season Wk 30-48	Postseason Wk 49-52	
15-point free throw game	X	X			43
17 drill		X			181
20-yard shuttle	X				14
300-yard shuttle	X	X	X		15, 180
30-second gassers		X	X		182
4, 8, 16 drill		X	X		181
55-second drill		X	X		184
Abdominal work	X	X	X		131-135
Back extension	X	X	X	X	165
Backboard slap and sprint		X	X		185
Backjack (ball handling)		X	X		202
Ball handling		X	X		201-204
Band work (rotator cuff)	X	X	X		142
Basketball and tennis ball dribble (ball handling		X	X		201
Basketball push-up	X	X	X		140
Bench press (dumbbell)	X	X	X		139
Bench step-up (single-leg)	X	X	X		154
Between-the-legs dribble (ball handling)		X	X		202
Biceps curl	X	X	X		146
Biceps/triceps work	X				145-147
Bleachers (ball handling)		X	X		202
Body blade		X			151
Body fat percentage (test)	X				12-13
Box jump-up	X	X			175

Exercise or drill name	Workout phase				Page # of exercise description
	Off-season Wk 1-21	Preseason Wk 22-29	In-season Wk 30-48	Postseason Wk 49-52	
Box squat	X	X	X		148
Chin-up	X		X	X	162
Circle pass		X			184
Close-grip bench press	X		X		159
Cone or minihurdle jumps		X			197-198
Core work			X	X	135-138
Crosscourt sprint and shoot		X	X		183
Crossover dribble (ball handling)		X	X		201
Crossover side step-up	X	X	X		153
Dip	X	X	X	X	138
Dot drills		X	X		190
Dumbbell bench press	X	X	X		139
Dumbbell fly	X	X			141
Dumbbell front shoulder raise	X	X	X		158
Dumbbell hammer curl	X	X	X		145
Dumbbell hammer curl to dumbbell push press			X		171
Dumbbell incline press	X	X	X		139
Dumbbell jump	X	X			173
Dumbbell leg curl	X	X	X		150
Dumbbell pullover	X				163
Dumbbell push-up, press, and twist		X			158
Dumbbell rear shoulder raise	X		X		159
Dumbbell side raise	X	X	X		157
Dumbbell split jump	X	X			175
Dumbbell squat thrust and jump		X			174
Dumbbell triceps extension	X	X			147
Dumbbell triceps kickback	X	X			146
External rotation (rotator cuff)	X	X	X		144
Finger count (ball handling)		X	X		203
Floor bench press	X	X	X		138
Four corner drill		X	X		182
Free throw golf			X		83
Gassers		X	X		181
Good morning	X	X	X		166
Half-court layup agility drill		X	X		193
Hang clean	X	X	X		163
Hang clean to front squat to push press	X		X		170

Exercise or drill name	Workout phase				Page # of exercise description
	Off-season Wk 1-21	Preseason Wk 22-29	In-season Wk 30-48	Postseason Wk 49-52	
Harness run		X	X		178
Heel raise	X	X	X		155
Height (test)	X				13
Hip abduction	X		X		151
Hip-up (ab work)	X	X	X		132
Home base		X	X		189
Inchworm (ab work)	X	X	X		135
Internal rotation (rotator cuff)	X	X	X		144
Jackknife (core work)			X	X	137
Jump rope routine		X	X		189
Knee raise (ab work)	X	X	X		131
Kneeling medicine ball chest pass					167
Knees to chest (ab work)	X	X	X		133
Ladder sprint		X	X		181
Lane agility box drill		X	X		192
Lane slide		X	X		193
Lat pull-down	X	X	X		160
Lateral box jump		X	X		176
Leg extension	X	X	X		149
Leg press	X	X	X		149
Light stretching	X	X	X	X	115-118
Lights out (ball handling)		X	X		203
Line drills (footwork)					191
Machine leg curl	X	X	X		151
Machine or cable row	X	X	X		163
Matrix I			X		172
Matrix II			X		172
Medicine ball backboard toss					168
Medicine ball chest pass	X	X	X		140
Medicine ball hold on Swiss ball (core work)		X	X	X	135
Medicine ball jump	X				174
Medicine ball pullover and throw	X	X			141
Medicine ball side raise (ab work)	X	X	X		132
Medicine ball sit-up throw (ab work)	X	X	X		133
Medicine ball squat press		X			169
Medicine ball squat throw		X			169

Exercise or drill name	Workout phase				Page # of exercise description
	Off-season Wk 1-21	Preseason Wk 22-29	In-season Wk 30-48	Postseason Wk 49-52	
Side lunge	X	X	X		152
Side squat	X		X		149
Side step-up	X				153
Sidewinder		X	X		177
Single-arm pullover		X	X		164
Single-leg balance (balance)					199
Single-leg bounding and balance triple jump (balance)					200
Single-leg dumbbell press	X		X		157
Single-leg medicine ball throw (medicine ball)					167
Single-leg short hop (balance)					200
Single-leg squat	X	X	X		148
Single-leg three-point floor touch (balance)					199
Single-leg vertical jump	X				176
Sit and reach (test)	X				13
Squat (front)	X	X	X		147
Sprint and walk ladder			X		186
Standing Swiss ball hug (core work)			X	X	136
Star agility drill		X			194
Straight-leg deadlift	X	X	X		147-148
Supraspinatus fly (rotator cuff)	X	X	X		143
Swiss ball balance push-up			X		140
Swiss ball bridge (core work)			X	X	136
Swiss ball chin-up	X	X	X		161
Swiss ball floor press		X			156
Swiss ball lat pull-down	X	X			161
Swiss ball leg curl	X	X	X		150
Swiss ball walkout push-up	X	X			139
T balance (balance)					199
T slide (footwork)					195
Team free throw and sprint			X		186
Tennis ball dribble (ball handling)		X	X		201
Tennis ball drop		X			197
Triangle slide		X			194
Triceps cable push-down	X	X	X		146
Two-ball dribble (ball handling)		X	X		204

Exercise or drill name	Workout phase				Page # of exercise description
	Off-season Wk 1-21	Preseason Wk 22-29	In-season Wk 30-48	Postseason Wk 49-52	
Uphill sprint		X			186
Upper ab crunch (ab work)	X	X	X		134
Vertical jump (test)	X				14
Viper jump		X			177
Walking lunge	X	X			152
Wall quick feet		X	X		178
Wall run		X	X		172, 180
Weight (test)	X				12

Year-Round Basketball Training

This book presents appropriate year-round training for both men and women players at the high school and college levels and aims to help the coach and athlete move beyond guesswork in designing a complete program that fits specific needs in all areas of conditioning. After years of having basketball coaches ask me how to train basketball players for peak performance and keep them in condition and injury free, it seemed time to answer all of those questions in a comprehensive year-round training guide. I have been in the strength and conditioning field for over 20 years and have worked with boys and girls at the junior and high school levels as well as men and women at the college and professional levels. My experience has allowed me to test many training systems and techniques and determine which ones translate most readily into success on the court.

My year-round training program for basketball incorporates eight distinct training phases throughout the four seasons of year. Each phase is designed to prepare you to reach your goals for that particular time of year. Table I.1 provides an overview of each phase as described here:

Off-Season I lasts eight weeks—seven weeks of basic strength and conditioning work to help prevent and protect the body from injury during workouts and the phases that follow, and one recovery week. This phase is a prerequisite for the explosive movement training to come. Basketball requires many explosive movements, and having a solid strength foundation is of the utmost importance in executing such movements.

Off-Season II lasts for six weeks—five weeks of slowly increasing conditioning and intensifying the resistance work and speed movements followed by one week of recovery. You must make the commitment to train while others fall by the "waist side." Success comes with a price of solid work during these summer months.

Off-Season III lasts seven weeks and benefits your game by introducing you to new sport-specific exercises and movements that help stimulate and create

Table 1.1 Workout Phases

Phase	Number of weeks	Focus	Chapter
Off-Season I	8	Laying the foundation	2
Off-Season II	6	Making the commitment	2
Off-Season III	7	Sport-specific conditioning	2
Preseason I	6	Preparing to play (skills and drills)	3
Preseason II	2	Training camp	3
In-Season I	13	Regular season, training to win	4
In-Season II	6	Tournament time	4
Postseason	4	Rest and recovery (physically and mentally)	5
TOTAL	52	Complete conditioning	

challenges for your body. Your conditioning becomes more specific to your game as training distances and times become shorter and movements become faster. This phase helps transfer the conditioning you've built in the early weeks of the off-season to the basketball court.

Preseason I takes you right to the court with six weeks of basketball skill work, drills, and conditioning. Everything that will enhance your game skills is systematically put into this phase. This is when you begin to get excited because you know that the start of practice is right around the corner.

Preseason II represents the first two weeks of official practice for most high school and college programs. This is what I refer to as training camp. Resistance work during this phase is cut back to give you more energy for your game, but your conditioning becomes more focused. The flexibility and stretching routines you adopted during off-season phases I and II will help keep your body fresh and free from injury.

In-Season I workouts train you to win games. Your training during this 13-week phase takes into account the frequency and intensity of games and balances this with the number of sets, reps, and percentages that you'll complete in training. Rest and recovery play an important role; neglecting them will have a negative effect on your game and your team.

In-Season II lasts for six weeks and is also known as tournament time. This is not the time to stop training, although you will want to cut back your intensity (workload) and volume (number of sets and reps) and even adjust your days of training. Your anaerobic power will be high in your resistance training and in your conditioning due to the in-season work you performed in the previous phase.

Postseason, or the rest and recovery phase, lasts four weeks and is designed to give you a physical and mental break after the season. Your body needs time to recover from the stresses of the game. The later weeks of this phase are designed to gradually get you back to training safely so that you can enter the next off-season cycle refreshed and healthy.

The five chapters in part I of this book cover the basic components of the basketball conditioning program as well as the specific workouts for each week of each phase described here.

CHAPTER 1

Program Components

Your body is an amazing machine. It actually uses different fuel tanks, or energy systems, depending on the duration and intensity of the activity you are performing. The key to any comprehensive sport-specific conditioning program is to train the appropriate energy system to the extent you will use it in performing that sport. The three energy systems used in basketball are the ATP-PCr system, the glycolytic system, and the aerobic system.

The ATP-PCr system is the system the body uses for activities lasting up to 30 seconds. For basketball players this includes activities such as dunking a basketball or sprinting down the court. Adenosine triphosphate (ATP) comes from a single molecule called phosphocreatine (PCr). Both ATP and PCr are chemical substances that are stored in the muscle cells for short-term bouts of energy. ATP that is broken down and used for energy is continuously being remade by energy released from the breakdown of PCr. The time it takes to replenish the ATP is mainly related to the recovery between bouts of exercises. This is why your recovery times and work-to-rest ratio times are so important. Training the body to replenish these supplies quickly is the main way you get into shape. You train this system by performing activities that require short bouts of energy such as short sprint work or weight training.

The *glycolytic,* or *anaerobic glycolysis, system* kicks in to supply energy needs of maximum efforts lasting from 30 to 90 seconds. For example, this is the energy system used for three to five continuous bouts of the 24-second clock in a fast-paced transition game. Thus, the way you train this system is by running 400-meter runs on a track, performing 45- to 90-second sprints on a stationary bike, or performing 45- to 90-second basketball drills.

The *aerobic,* or *oxidative, system* is what your body relies on after 90 seconds of activity. When the ATP-PCr and glycolytic systems produce energy, they also produce a by-product called lactic acid. This by-product is produced when no oxygen is present, just as ash is a by-product from a fire. The aerobic system, on the other hand, can provide energy for the body for longer periods because no fatiguing by-products (such as lactic acid) are produced in the presence of oxygen. Training the aerobic system requires performing activities such as an 800-meter run (two laps on a standard track) or a drill such as the *rim touch* (see page 183) that lasts for a continuous 90 seconds or more.

Figure 1.1 highlights these systems.

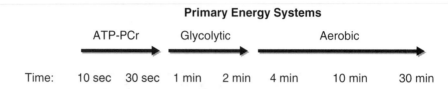

Figure 1.1 The three energy systems used in basketball.

Because basketball requires short bursts of powerful movements, it is primarily anaerobic. The game does have an aerobic component, however, since the anaerobic movements are needed over a longer period—over the course of a game. Each week of the 52-week program trains the body for the specific needs of basketball through proper warm-ups, flexibility training, resistance training, basketball-specific conditioning, and skill training.

Warm-Ups and Flexibility Training

Take the time to warm the muscles before stressing them with a workout and to reduce the risk of injury. The warm-up and flexibility programs I recommend for resistance work are a bit different from the ones I recommend for conditioning work. Both, however, center on increasing circulation in the entire body and focus on the major muscle groups used in basketball: the chest, shoulders, lower back, pelvis and hips, hamstrings and quadriceps in the upper leg, and gastrocnemius and Achilles tendon in the lower leg.

Resistance Training Warm-Up

I recommend a warm-up period of 2 to 10 minutes of aerobic work, such as jumping rope for 2 to 3 minutes, riding a stationary bike or running on a treadmill for 5 to 10 minutes, or performing calisthenics for 2 minutes, before starting any resistance work. Follow this warm-up with 5 to 10 minutes of stretching.

Another great way to warm up before starting resistance work is to work the abdominal muscles first. This helps you warm up the core of the body along with the muscles of the lower back. When you increase circulation and body temperature in these two areas first, your body responds better and faster to warming up other parts.

Using stretching bands to stretch lightly before upper body weight training and after your warm-up can help increase flexibility in the chest and shoulders. Light stretching before a leg resistance workout should focus on the muscles of the hips, quads, and hamstrings. These muscles are some of the biggest muscles of the body, so you must not neglect them. Chapter 6 provides various flexibility exercises that are appropriate for the upper and lower body, as well as an explanation of how to perform (and how long to hold) each stretch.

After each weight training or conditioning workout you should take 8 to 10 minutes to stretch again. This will help prevent lactic acid build-up and help recovery.

Conditioning Warm-Up

A warm-up for a conditioning workout should last anywhere from 5 to 10 minutes and include movements called dynamic stretches or running warm-ups. Running warm-ups are a series of running drills that increase circulation and stretch the areas of the hips, hamstrings, quads, and calves.

If you are outdoors on a field or track, make sure you have 35 to 40 yards on which to do each running warm-up. If you are on a basketball court, perform each drill from baseline to baseline.

1. **Heel-toe.** Walk at a normal pace, but with each foot landing, come down on your heel and then lift up as high as possible on your toes. (This warms up the calf muscles.)
2. **Walk in the snow.** Start by walking and bringing one knee up high and out to the side and back down. Repeat with the other leg. Move as if you were walking in deep snow. (This is a great hip warm-up.)
3. **Russian march and butt kick.** Start by walking and bringing your leg up as high as possible with only a slight bend in the knee and repeat as though you were marching. Follow this by a length in which you lean forward and bring your heels back to your buttocks. (The Russian march is a good hamstring stretch, and the butt kicks balance that with quadriceps work.)
4. **Backward walk and reach.** Walk backward as if you were kicking someone behind you in the chest. Lean forward each time you kick your leg back. It is not a forceful kick but a nice and easy extension of the leg. (This warms up the hamstring muscles.)
5. **Backward run.** Run backward, being sure to get up high on the balls of your feet. (This is a good warm-up for calf muscles and the Achilles tendon.)
6. **High knee pump.** When running, bring each knee up to your waist and repeat with a nice and easy rhythm. (This is a great quad stretch.)
7. **Power skip.** Perform an easy skipping motion, but bring each knee up to waist level each time. (This works the quadriceps and hips.)
8. **Carioca.** Run sideways by crossing each foot in front of the body then bringing it behind you as the other foot goes in front. Hold your arms out to the side to help turn the hips. (This is good for loosening up the pelvis area.)
9. **Tight S.** Run a tight S pattern. (This is great for warming up and preventing injuries to the ankles and knees.)
10. **1-2-3-4-5-cut.** Run five steps to the right at 45 degrees; then cut and plant with the right foot. Then run five steps to the left at 45 degrees and plant with the left foot. Repeat down the length of the court.
11. **Defensive power slide shuffle.** Shuffle 45 degrees to the right, then to the left. Keep your arms out, knees bent, and hips down.

A good warm-up before a training camp practice or hard practice during the in-season involves a contrast warm-up, which alternates the dynamic movements just listed with stretches from chapter 6 as in the following:

1. Heel-toe followed by knees side to side (10 seconds)
2. Russian march followed by quadriceps stretch (90 seconds)
3. Butt kick followed by hamstring stretch (90 seconds)
4. Power slide shuffle followed by groin stretch (90 seconds)
5. Carioca followed by ankle inversion and calf stretch (90 seconds)

Be creative by mixing running warm-ups and stretching in many different ways. Go from running warm-ups to stretching and back to running warm-ups as quickly as possible. Make it fun!

Photo courtesy of the Charlotte Sting

Dawn Staley knows the importance of a proper warm-up.

Resistance Training

Force, power, and strength are necessary components for good basketball.

$$\text{Force} = \text{mass} \times \text{acceleration}$$

$$\text{Power} = \text{force} \times \text{velocity}$$

$$\text{Strength} = \text{speed} \times \text{power}$$

Building strength, force, and power is the purpose of resistance training. The year-round training program is designed to give you maximum power, force, strength, speed, and other benefits from resistance training at the right time of the season.

The year-round resistance work starts with off-season weight workouts three days a week—Monday, Wednesday, and Friday (see chapter 2), alternating upper body workouts with lower body workouts. That is, one week you work the upper body twice and the lower body once and the next week you work the lower body twice and the upper body once. Alternating workouts in this way keeps the joints fresh and strong and prevents burnout and fatigue.

During the preseason phase you continue with three resistance workouts per week, but each day has set workouts (see chapter 3). Monday and Friday focus on strengthening the chest, legs, and arms, whereas Wednesday is devoted to back and shoulder work. During training camp (the first two weeks of practice) you do total body workouts on Tuesdays and Thursdays only; in the in-season (see chapter 4) you continue with resistance training twice a week, each session being a total body workout.

Intensity and the One Repetition Maximum

Basketball players don't have to be big or able to lift a heavy bench press to be successful. Functional strength, or how you use the strength for what is required during the game, is what is important. Some athletes, both men and women, may want to put on weight or gain strength to do battle under the boards or jump higher. In this book special sets for these athletes are denoted by PW (power work). Other athletes may have plenty of strength and size, but may want to increase speed and remain toned by keeping their body fat down. Special sets for these individuals are noted by SW (speed work). Still other athletes may be beginners to the sport or to lifting weights and may need to start off with the lighter weights to safely grow accustomed to what their bodies can withstand during the first year. Whatever your current level and needs, the right resistance training workouts can help you. Chapters 2 through 5 explain how to individualize workouts for your needs.

Regardless of the intensity of the lift, you should focus on your form, technique, and speed of movement. Perform any resistance training exercise with controlled speed, no matter how heavy or light the weight. Keep in mind that with the lighter lifts, a beginner or advanced athlete can focus more on the controlled explosiveness of the movement without worrying about putting on too much mass or unwanted bulk. This has always been the concern of many athletes I have worked with from high school to professional players.

In each workout, the intensity of each lift is noted using percentage of one repetition maximum (or % 1RM). For example, 3 × 10 (70 to 75%) means three sets of 10 repetitions each at 70 to 75% of your repetition maximum for that lift.

There are several ways to determine your 1RM. Each athlete should do so for the bench press, push press, and squat or leg press exercises to establish a starting point on which to base all other lifts during the season. For some high school girls and first-year high school boys, I recommend testing strength levels by performing a "predicted max," as I have found over the years that the predicted max is much safer and easier on the shoulders than a 1RM and just as accurate. The muscular endurance and strength you obtain from the predicted max is far more beneficial than trying to lift a heavy object just one time. This is a safe, effective, and accurate way of finding your 1RM without actually having to perform a 1RM test.

To find your predicted max:

1. Perform one warm-up set of 8 to 10 repetitions using only the bar. If you are testing on the leg press, use just the carriage.

2. Rest for two minutes.

3. Perform a second set of five repetitions of light resistance (around 60% of what you estimate your max to be).

4. Rest for three minutes.

5. Perform a third set of three repetitions using medium weight (75% of your estimated max).

6. Rest for three minutes.

7. Perform a last set of three to eight reps in an all-out effort (85 to 90% of your max).

8. Use table 1.1 to find your predicted max. For example, if you find that you are able to do five repetitions of lifting 280 pounds (127 kilograms) on the bench press, divide 280 by .857 to get your predicted max of 327 pounds (148 kilograms) for the bench press.

Table 1.1 Finding Your Predicted Maximum

Number of repetitions	Percentage
1	1.00
2	.955
3	.917
4	.885
5	.857
6	.832
7	.809
8	.788
9	.769
10	.752
11	.736
12	.721

9. Perform the same test for the push press and for the squat or leg press.

Try to stay within two to eight reps when testing your predicted max. Any more than eight reps tests your muscular endurance instead of muscular strength.

A second way for beginner to intermediate athletes to find their 1RM is to use a progress protocol as follows:

1. Warm up with light resistance, 5 to 10 reps.

2. Rest for one minute.

3. Add 10 to 20 pounds (4.5 to 9 kilograms) for upper body exercises (bench press and push press). Add 30 to 40 pounds (13.6 to 18 kilograms) for lower body exercises (squat or leg press).

4. Rest for two minutes.

5. Add 10 to 20 pounds for upper body exercises. Add 30 to 40 pounds for lower body exercises.

6. Rest for two to four minutes.

7. Add 10 to 20 pounds for upper body exercises. Add 30 to 40 pounds for lower body exercises.

8. Attempt a 1RM lift.

9. If you are successful at the 1RM lift, rest for two to four minutes and repeat steps 7 through 9. If you are unsuccessful, rest two to four minutes and decrease the load by subtracting 5 to 10 pounds (2.3 to 4.5 kilograms) from upper body exercises and 15 to 20 pounds (6.8 to 9 kilograms) from lower body exercises and repeat step 8.

Ideally, the athlete's 1RM is measured within the first five testing steps.

I suggest that advanced athletes (both women and men) find their max from percentages. Most athletes at this level have a pretty good guess of what they can and cannot do, so finding their max from estimated percentages is a good and accurate way of testing.

First set—very light warm-up set of five to eight reps

Second set—use 50% of estimated max for five reps

Third set—use 65% for three reps

Fourth set—use 85% for two reps

Fifth set—all-out effort for 1RM

On some workout days you will naturally feel weaker than on other days. When this is the case, try not to reduce the recommended percentage you lift; rather, reduce the number of repetitions as needed. If you feel stronger on a particular day and your squat or leg press workout calls for three sets of five at 80% of your max (240 pounds or 109 kilograms) when your 1RM is 300 pounds, add five pounds to your max (now 305 pounds or 138 kilograms) and take the percentage of that new max. Your workout now will call for three sets of five reps at 245 pounds each. Be sure to record your new maximum in your training log. The importance of keeping a training log is discussed later in the chapter.

Functional Balance and Stability

From time to time throughout the workout phases you will see workouts that call for work on a Swiss ball, balance pad, or body blade. These exercises are designed to help create stability and balance (sometimes known as proprioception) in the ankle, knee, and core. In basketball you must be able to control different unstable movements while still executing the play, shot, or rebound. You will perform these drills during the latter part of the off-season, during the preseason, and moderately during the in-season. Adding a balance and stability component to lifts is also a great way to help prevent injuries at the ankle, knee, and shoulder joints. If you do not have access to a balance pad, then you may stand on one leg while performing a particular exercise to help create imbalance and instability. Some exercises call for single-leg movements as a prerequisite to exercises that call for training aids such as balance pads or body blades.

Workout Partners

A workout partner or teammate can be very beneficial. Choose someone your own age or at your strength level who also has some of the same goals as a basketball player that you do. This can make off-season workouts in particular more fun and competitive. It is also great for motivation when you don't really "have it" on a given day; you may be able to pick each other up in so many different ways. Remember that success doesn't come easy and that winning is the hardest thing you'll ever have to accomplish.

Differences Between Male and Female Athletes

Upper body strength, on average, is considerably less in females than in males. This difference can be largely related to anatomical and physiological differences. Studies, however, show a variation in the amount of differences. Total body absolute strength of female athletes is only about two-thirds that of their male counterparts, and the absolute strength of the upper body is even less. Note, though, that the female athlete has proportionally the same muscular energy stored as her male counterpart, and studies have shown that when performance depends on energy storage capacity, the female's strength is closer to the male's.

Because female athletes have wider hips, they may have a tendency to rotate the upper leg inward when performing leg presses or squats. Keeping the toes pointed straight and the knees directly over the feet when performing these two exercises can correct this. Females also tend to have a weaker vastus medialis (located inside the upper leg muscle) than their male counterparts. Strengthening the muscles, ligaments, and tendons surrounding the knee joint should provide the extra stability that the female athlete needs. While performing leg extensions, female athletes should point the toes outward and place the pad on the inside of the ankle. This will help strengthen the weaker muscle of the upper leg (vastus medialis).

Conditioning and Skill Training

The game of basketball is a collection of short stop-and-go sprints combined with change-of-direction movements (agility) and vertical jumps. A basketball-specific conditioning program incorporates these different types of training and training aids to allow you to be at your top fitness level throughout the season. To help you reach the top fitness levels, each conditioning workout has (depending on the time of year) a component of conditioning that may include the following:

- Middle-distance running (off-season) at a track or baseball field
- Sprint work (off-season, preseason, and in-season) at a track, a basketball court, or in the shallow end of a pool
- Agility work and footwork drills (off-season, preseason) on the court
- Plyometrics (off-season) on a basketball court or any soft but stable surface
- Resistant exercises using tubing for sprinting and jumping (preseason) on the court

Chapters 8 and 9 provide specific exercises and drills for each of these components.

Make sure that you are properly warmed up before beginning any conditioning, speed, agility, or explosive movement workout. The running warm-ups and stretching exercises are a part of each running and jumping program, with 10 minutes allotted for each.

Getting conditioned for basketball depends a lot on the rest, also known as recovery, you take between each running set. The duration of the recovery time is always related to the distance of the run or sprint, plus the time it takes to complete it. The work you perform and the rest time that follows is known as the work-to-rest ratio. A usual work-to-rest ratio is 1:1, 1:2, or 1:3; that is, the rest is one, two, or three times the duration that it takes to perform the sprint. As a general rule, the higher the intensity of the work, the greater the rest you should get so that you can fully recover between each set. Any sprint that is less than 30 seconds requires a 1:3 or 1:2 work-to-rest ratio. For example, a 20-second sprint should be followed by a 40- to 60-second rest interval. Sprints that last 30 to 90 seconds should have between a 1:2 and 1:3 work-to-rest ratio. Sprints from 90 to 180 seconds need a work-to-rest ratio of 1:1 or 1:2 (see table 1.2).

Table 1.2 Times, Distance, and Work-to-Rest Ratios

Work time (seconds)	Distance (yards)	Work-to-rest ratio
0-30	0-220	1:2 to 1:3
30-90	220-660	1:2 to 1:3
90-180	660-1,320	1:1 to 1:2

CHECKING YOUR HEART RATE

The intensity at which you condition or run can be measured by checking your exercise heart rate. You do this by locating your pulse at your carotid artery (in your neck). Simply place the tips of your index and middle fingers gently over this site. When you locate your heartbeat, count your pulse for 10 seconds. Then, multiply that number by six and you will have an estimate of your heart rate for one minute (measured in beats per minute, bpm). You can also count your pulse for 15 seconds and multiply that number by four. This may give you a more accurate reading.

In chapter 2, which addresses your off-season program, I have designed different treadmill workouts starting at a very low intensity for fat burning to a very high intensity for sport-specific conditioning. During these workouts, it is important to check your heart rate to see if you are in the particular desired training zone and if you can hold that heart rate or training zone over a certain time or over a certain distance. As you continue to train, you will be able to reach and hold a higher training heart rate. It is much like strength training in that a progression in intensity is a must to create the physical improvements you desire.

The treadmill or stepper workouts may call for you to train between 60 and 85% of your maximum heart rate depending on the intended intensity of the workout. To find this training zone, you must first determine your maximum heart rate. One of the easiest ways to estimate this is to simply subtract your age from 220. For example, an 18-year-old basketball player would have an age-predicted maximum heart rate of 202 beats per minute (220 – 18 = 202). Once you determine your maximum, you can determine your training heart rate. If the workout on the treadmill or stepper calls for you to train between 75 and 80% for 20 minutes, you would simply use the formula of 202 beats per minute and multiply that by .75 and .80:

$$202 \times .75 = 151 \text{ bpm; and } 202 \text{ bpm} \times .80 = 161 \text{ bpm.}$$

So your training zone at 75 to 80% maximum heart rate would be between 151 and 161 beats per minute.

You can also check your heart rate after exercises such as a 10- to 15-repetition squat set or a 100-yard sprint. It's fun to see how fast your heart has been pumping during exercise.

Program Testing

It is important that you keep records of your progress during the year by periodically going through a series of tests that measure your body weight, percentage of body fat, flexibility, vertical jump, leg strength, upper body strength, agility, speed, and endurance. Having a record of each test will help you see areas in which you are improving.

Perform these tests at least three times a year—at the beginning of the off-season, at the beginning of the preseason, and a few days before the beginning of your first day of practice. A coach or trainer who is familiar with each testing procedure should help administer each test. Spread the testing over two separate days to provide your body with a rest.

Day 1	**Day 2**
Height without shoes _____	Sit and reach _____
with shoes ____	Vertical jump _____ (no step)
Body weight ____	20-yard shuttle run _____
Body fat % _____	300-yard shuttle run _____
Bench press max ____	
Push press max _____	
Squat or leg press max ____	

Height and Weight

Measure your height and weight at the beginning of the season and periodically during the year. When taking height and weight measurements, record them with your shoes on and with your shoes off. (These are the measurements most colleges and even the pro recruiters want to know. Be sure to point your toes out and place your heels together and against the wall for accurate and consistent height measurements.)

Body Fat Percentage

Extra body fat can hamper play by slowing speed and acceleration and impairing jumping ability. That's why it is so important to test body fat percentages when possible. Perhaps the most accurate way to check body fat is by underwater weighing; however, this requires some very elaborate equipment, and the cost can be very expensive. Unless your school has access to such equipment, use an easier, less expensive method: skin-fold calipers. Because using the calipers accurately requires specific training, an athletic trainer, physical education teacher, strength and conditioning coach, or other professional should perform the test.

Going under the guidelines listed in table 1.3 can to some degree be unhealthy. Having some body fat is important for daily functions; it provides joint support and the energy that you need for long bouts of training and playing ball. Keep in mind also that the ideal body compositions of men and women are different; biologically, women tend to store more fat than men. Men also tend to have more muscle mass (40%) than women (23%). These differences in muscle mass help explain the general differences in strength levels between men and women.

Table 1.3 Ideal Body Fat Composition Ranges by Position

Position	Male (%)	Female (%)
Center	10-12	18-20
Power forward	9.5-11	17-19
Small forward	9-10	16-18
Shooting guard	7.5-8.5	15-17
Point guard	6.5-8	14-16

Flexibility—Sit and Reach

The sit and reach test measures flexibility of the lower back and hamstrings. A piece of equipment called the sit and reach box records the measurement; if one is not available, a ruler or yardstick will do the job.

1. Sit with your legs extended in front of you with your feet three to six inches apart. The soles of your feet should touch the bottom step of a flight of stairs.

2. Put a ruler on the first step so that it hangs over the step in your direction. The inch mark on the ruler that marks the soles of your feet will be zero for the testing. Reaching beyond your feet indicates positive numbers. Not being able to reach your feet is a negative number.

3. Keep your knees locked. With your hands together, palms down, and your chin on your chest, exhale as you bend slowly forward from the waist. Reach out as far as you can beyond your toes; then hold for one to two seconds. Repeat two more times and record your best score.

Strength Test

Use one of the methods described on pages 7 to 9 to periodically test your strength for the bench press, push press, and squat or leg press. Remember that if you increase the maximum you can lift during one of these periodic tests, you should update the percentage maximum you lift for each subsequent workout.

Vertical Jump Test

The vertical jump test is a great way to measure explosive power of the lower body. First find your standing reach by standing sideways against a wall. Mark your fingertips with chalk. Reach as high as possible while standing with both feet flat on the ground and make a chalk mark on the wall. Then tape a yardstick to the wall, matching the bottom of the yardstick to the chalk mark. From the chalk mark, the yardstick should be pointed toward the ceiling.

When this is completed, rechalk your fingertips, stand sideways against the wall, and jump as high as you can, topping the yardstick at your highest point of the jump. Do not take a step before jumping. Your feet should be directly under your armpits when jumping. Jump three times, and record your best jump.

Agility Test—20-Yard Shuttle

The 20-yard shuttle helps measures your agility (how fast you change direction), acceleration, and deceleration. To perform the test, do the following:

1. Measure five yards in each direction from center court. Mark these spots with tape.

2. Straddle the centerline with your feet at equal distance from the centerline.

3. On command from your coach or partner, run in either direction toward the line and touch it with your hand.

4. Change direction and run toward the opposite line and touch it also with your hand.

5. Change direction once again and run through the center. When your chest crosses the centerline, the drill is over. Record the best of two to three trials, and check these against table 1.4.

Table 1.4 20-Yard Shuttle Test Scoring

	Females (time in seconds)	Males (time in seconds)
Excellent	<4.5	<4.0
Good	4.6-5.1	4.1-4.6
Fair	5.2-5.8	4.7-5.3
Poor	>5.9	>5.4

Anaerobic Endurance—300-Yard Shuttle

The 300-yard shuttle run helps measure your anaerobic endurance and is performed as follows:

1. Measure and mark 25 yards on a track or gym floor.
2. Sprint to the 25-yard mark, touch it with your foot, then turn and sprint back to the starting line. Repeat this six times without stopping.
3. Rest five minutes and repeat.
4. Check your scores against those in table 1.5.

Table 1.5 300-Yard Shuttle Test Scoring

	Females (time in seconds)	Males (time in seconds)
Excellent	<50.9	<45.9
Good	51-59.9	46-50.9
Fair	60-64.9	51-54.9
Poor	>65	>55

If you are weak in one or more areas of the testing, then it is important to concentrate and work harder on that particular area in your year-round training. If, however, you score well on a particular test, you'll want to continue to work hard in that area to excel to an even greater degree. Anytime you can become better or more efficient at a particular drill or test, you are taking advantage of an opportunity to become a better athlete. It's all about becoming the best that you can be!

Laying the Foundation: Off-Season Workouts

The off-season phase begins immediately after your four weeks of postseason work (see chapter 5). The off-season includes three separate phases totaling 21 weeks, three of which are rest and recovery weeks. The goal of your training throughout these three phases is to develop the fitness base that is a prerequisite to the sport-specific training that occurs later in the season.

Off-Season Phase I

Phase I of the off-season work is eight weeks long—seven weeks of basic strength work on Mondays, Wednesdays, and Fridays and aerobic conditioning on Tuesdays and Thursdays, followed by one week of recovery. This phase of conditioning involves low-intensity training. If you want to drop a few pounds, getting up early in the morning to do some treadmill work is a great way to get rid of unwanted body fat. Training early in the morning helps speed up your metabolic rate so that you burn calories more efficiently throughout the day.

If you wish, you can combine the conditioning workouts to go with your weight training work on Mondays, Wednesdays, or Fridays. For example, you can do Tuesday's conditioning workout after Monday's weight training workout or even early that morning before school or work. You can then do Thursday's conditioning work on Wednesday or Friday after the weight training or early in the morning. If you decide to combine weight training and conditioning workouts into a single session on a given day, I suggest that you do your weight training first. In this way, your conditioning work will not leave you fatigued for your weight training.

Resistance Training

To keep athletes from burning out, I have designed the program to have different workouts from one phase to another. For example, phase I of the off-season lasts eight weeks, and athletes alternate between workout 1 (chest, shoulders, and triceps) and workout 2 (legs, hips, back, and biceps). So, during the first week, if you start with workout 2 on Monday, and do workout 1 Wednesday and workout 2 Friday, the next Monday you will start with workout 1. This is a great way to keep the joints fresh and strong, which is important in any sport but especially in basketball.

Throughout phase I athletes follow a periodization model. The first four weeks concentrate on high repetitions and hypertrophy (muscle development) work that is the beginning of basic strength and power. The high repetitions are the first step in laying the foundation of the off-season program. Hypertrophy work not only builds muscle, but also helps stabilize joints. Too often, young high school or college athletes start off weight training by performing low reps and heavy weight without the proper muscular structure to lift, control, and balance the resistance. Using high reps will ensure that you start with the right amount of weight to prevent injury.

The training loads start at 65 to 70% of one repetition max (1RM) for both male and female athletes. All sets in this phase are geared toward both power and speed work unless otherwise noted. When specific sets are designated as PW (power work), those are for players who want to put on size and mass. Players who don't want extra size and strength should use the SW (speed work) sets.

Before starting your off-season workouts, take some time to get your off-season testing in (see testing details at the end of chapter 1). Checking your progress at this point and then again during the preseason will tell you your maximums on the core lifts (bench press, push press, and squat or leg press) and help you determine the workloads for your exercises.

Throughout phase I of the off-season you have three work sets (sets that exclude warm-up sets). Warm-up sets are used for all core lifts such as the bench press, push press, squat, and leg press. These sets are anywhere between 45 and 50% of your 1RM on that particular exercise. Other auxiliary exercises do not require a warm-up set since the exercise sequence starts with the larger-muscle groups first in the workout, followed by the smaller-muscle groups. Thus the larger-muscle lifts warm up the body and supply adequate blood flow for the smaller-muscle lifts. The percentage progressions on some exercises also help in the warm-up process to a large degree. If you feel you should warm up with a lighter weight on an exercise such as a barbell curl before a set, please do so.

During phase I of the off-season you are introduced to supersets, denoted by SS next to the exercise. Supersets are two back-to-back exercises that use the same body part; you take little or no rest between them. Supersets put more stress on the body's nervous system and are really great for shaping, toning, and speeding up the metabolic process (i.e., the amount of calories you are burning while in a resting state). Combination sets, denoted by CS, are the same as supersets except that you train different body parts.

Beginning lifters may choose to lift lighter weight for the reps prescribed and not follow the percentages that are designated in the table. Although this method involves more trial and error, it may be more comfortable for a beginning lifter.

All resistance training exercises listed in the following workouts are detailed in chapter 7.

Conditioning

Conditioning at this point in the season is for those who want or need to lose some extra body fat or for those who simply want to stay more aerobically active during this time of year. This conditioning period focuses more on aerobic work on the treadmill, stair-stepper, or any other type of cardiovascular equipment that you might like as well as running outside or riding a bike. I've drawn up a conditioning workout for two days a week (typically on days on which you do not lift weights, Tuesdays and Thursdays). Be sure to adhere to the heart rate workloads I prescribe when conditioning during this time. These will guide you in progressive workloads to keep you from overtraining or doing too much work too soon. Chapter 1 (pages 11 to 12) describes how to find your heart rate max and monitor your heart rate.

Skill Training

No basketball skill work is required during phase I of the off-season. Of course, with the arrival of spring and higher temperatures I suggest getting outside for a pickup game or just getting out to put up some shots whenever possible. You'll be surprised at the improvements you can make in your game by spending time under the goal in your backyard or on the court at your local park.

The summer months are also a good time to have fun learning how to juggle. This can be done with tennis balls or beanbags. Start off with two; then move to three tennis balls or beanbags when you feel comfortable. Juggling is great for improving hand-eye coordination, and you will see the results in your ball-handling skills once the season starts.

Off-season training pays off at game time for players at all levels. Pictured here is Elden Campbell; he now plays for the Seattle Supersonics.

Week 1   **Off-Season**

MONDAY

Testing

See chapter 1, pages 12 to 15 for procedures.

Height with and without shoes

Weight and body fat percentage

Bench press

Push press

Squat or leg press

TUESDAY

Testing

See chapter 1, pages 12 to 15 for procedures.

Sit and reach

Vertical jump

20-yard shuttle

300-yard shuttle

WEDNESDAY

Resistance training

EXERCISE	SETS × REPS (% 1RM)
Abdominal work	Choose 4 exercises × 20 to 30 (pages 131 to 135).
Light stretching	5 minutes
Rotator cuff work	Choose 1 exercise × 8 to 10 (pages 142 to 144).
Bench press	3 × 10 (65, 70, 70%)
Dumbbell incline press	3 × 10 (65 to 70%)
Push press (bar)	3 × 10 (65, 70, 70%)
Triceps cable push-down	3 × 10 to 15 (65 to 70%)
Dumbbell pullover	2 × 10 (65 to 70%)

THURSDAY

Conditioning

Low-intensity aerobic activity for 20 to 30 minutes (65% max heart rate—see chapter 1, pages 11 to 12 for guidelines on checking your heart rate).

Stretch 10 minutes.

FRIDAY

Resistance training

EXERCISE	SETS × REPS (% 1RM OR INTENSITY)
Abdominal work	Choose 4 exercises × 20 to 30.
Light stretching	5 minutes
Leg extension	2 × 10 to 12 (70 to 75%)
Squat or leg press	3 × 10 (65, 70, 70%)
Machine leg curl	3 × 10 (70 to 75%)
Lat pull-down (SS)	3 × 10 (75 to 80%)
Power shrug (dumbbell) (SS)	3 × 10 (70 to 75%)
Back extension	3 × 15
Heel raise	4 × 10 to 12 (70 to 75%)

Week 2 Off-Season

MONDAY

Resistance training

EXERCISE	SETS × REPS (% 1RM OR INTENSITY)
Abdominal work	Choose 4 exercises × 20 to 30.
Light stretching	5 minutes
Rotator cuff work	Choose 1 exercise × 8 to 10.
Bench press	3 × 10 (65, 70, 75%)
Dip	3 × to failure
Push press (dumbbell alternating)	3 × 10 (70 to 75%)
Dumbbell pullover	3 × 10 (75 to 80%)
Dumbbell kickback	3 × 10 (70 to 75%)

TUESDAY

Conditioning

Low-intensity aerobic activity for 30 to 40 minutes (65% max heart rate).

Stretch 10 minutes.

WEDNESDAY

Resistance training

EXERCISE	SETS × REPS (% 1RM OR INTENSITY)
Abdominal work	Choose 4 exercises × 20 to 30.
Light stretching	5 minutes
Leg extension	2 × 10 to 12 (70 to 75%)
Squat or leg press	3 × 10 (65, 70, 75%)
Machine leg curl	3 × 10 (75 to 80%)
Machine row (SS)	3 × 10 (70 to 75%)
Power shrug (bar) (SS)	3 × 10 (70 to 75%)
Back extension	3 × 15
Heel raise	4× 10 to 12 (70 to 75%)

THURSDAY

Conditioning

Do the following in the shallow end of the pool (from side to side). Water should be waist high. You may also use an aqua vest during this workout.

Warm up with one lap of each of the following:

- Walk in the snow
- Heel-toe walk
- Russian march
- Butt kick
- Backward walk and reach
- Power skip
- High knee pump
- Carioca
- Tight S
- Power slide right – left

Workout:

- Double-leg bound across pool
- Vertical jump 1 × 8
- Single-leg vertical jump 3 × 6
- Sprint work 2 × 6
- Run in place with high knee pumps (for speed) 3 × 15 seconds

Cool down with a relaxing swim.

Week 2 *(continued)*

FRIDAY

Resistance training	
EXERCISE	**SETS × REPS (% 1RM OR INTENSITY)**
Abdominal work	Choose 4 exercises × 20 to 30.
Light stretching	5 minutes
Dumbbell incline press	3 × 10 (70 to 75%)
Dumbbell fly	3 × 10 (70 to 75%)
Push press (SS)	3 × 10 (70 to 75%)
Dumbbell front shoulder raise (SS)	2 × 10 (70 to 75%)
Triceps cable push-down	3 × 10 (70 to 75%)

Week 3 **Off-Season**

MONDAY

Resistance training

EXERCISE	SETS × REPS (% 1RM OR INTENSITY)
Abdominal work	Choose 4 exercises × 20 to 30.
Light stretching	5 minutes
Leg extension	3 × 10 to 12 (70 to 75%)
Single-leg squat	3 × 10 each leg (70 to 75%)
Straight-leg deadlift (SS)	3 × 10 (70 to 75%)
Side step-up (SS)	3 × 8 each side (10- to 25-lb dumbbell)
Hang clean	3 × 8 (70 to 75%)
Lat pull-down	3 × 10 (70 to 75%)
Dumbbell hammer curl (standing)	3 × 10 (70 to 75%)
Heel raise	4 × 10 (70 to 75%)

TUESDAY

Conditioning

Low-intensity aerobic activity for 30 to 40 minutes (70% max heart rate).

Stretch 10 minutes.

WEDNESDAY

Resistance training

EXERCISE	SETS × REPS (% 1RM OR INTENSITY)
Abdominal work	Choose 4 exercises × 20 to 30.
Light stretching	5 minutes
Rotator cuff work	Choose 1 exercise × 8 to 10.
Bench press	3 × 10 (65, 70, 75%)
Push-up	2 × 10
Seated row press	3 × 10 (75 to 80%)
Dumbbell rear shoulder raise	2 × 10 (70 to 75%)
Dumbbell kickback	3 × 10 (70 to 75%)

THURSDAY

Conditioning

Do the following in the shallow end of the pool (from side to side). Water should be waist high. You may also use an aqua vest during this workout.

Warm up with one lap of each of the following:

- Walk in the snow
- Heel-toe walk
- Russian march
- Butt kick
- Backward walk and reach
- Power skip
- High knee pump
- Carioca
- Tight S
- Power slide right – left

Workout:

- Double-leg bound across pool
- Vertical jump 1 × 8
- Run in place with high knee pumps (for speed) 3 × 15 seconds
- Single-leg vertical jump 3 × 6
- Sprint work 2 × 6

Cool down with a relaxing swim.

Week 3 *(continued)*

Resistance training	
EXERCISE	**SETS × REPS (% 1RM OR INTENSITY)**
Abdominal work	Choose 4 exercises × 20 to 30.
Light stretching	5 minutes
Leg press	3 × 10 (65, 70, 75%)
Hip abduction (tubing) (SS)	3 × 10 each leg
Dumbbell leg curl (SS)	3 × 10 (70 to 75%)
Lat pull-down	3 × 10 (75 to 80%)
Biceps curl	3 × 10 (70 to 75%)
Back extension	3 × 15 to 20
Heel raise	4 × 10 (75 to 80%)

FRIDAY

Week 4 **Off-Season**

MONDAY

Resistance training	
EXERCISE	**SETS × REPS (% 1RM OR INTENSITY)**
Abdominal work	Choose 4 exercises × 20 to 30.
Light stretching	5 minutes
Rotator cuff work	Choose 1 exercise × 8 to 10.
Floor bench press	3 × 10 (75 to 80%)
Close-grip bench press (SS)	3 × 8 (75 to 80%)
Push press (SS)	3 × 8 (65, 70, 75%)
Dumbbell side raise (CS)	3 × 8 (70 to 75%)
Triceps cable push-down (CS)	3 × 10 to 15 (70 to 75%)

TUESDAY

Conditioning

Low-intensity aerobic activity for 35 to 45 minutes (65 to 70% max heart rate).
Stretch 10 minutes.

WEDNESDAY

Resistance training	
EXERCISE	**SETS × REPS (% 1RM OR INTENSITY)**
Abdominal work	Choose 4 exercises × 20 to 30.
Light stretching	5 minutes
Leg extension	3 × 10 to 12 (70 to 75%)
Squat or leg press (SS)	3 × 10 (65, 70, 75%)
Crossover side step-up (SS)	3 × 10 (25-lb dumbbells)
Machine leg curl	3 × 8 (75 to 80%)
Hang clean	3 × 8 (70 to 75%)
Dumbbell hammer curl	3 × 8 (70 to 75%)
Heel raise	4 × 10 (75 to 80%)
Reverse hyperextension	3 × 15 to 20

THURSDAY

Conditioning

Low-intensity aerobic activity for 35 to 45 minutes (65 to 70% max heart rate).
Stretch 10 minutes.

FRIDAY

Resistance training	
EXERCISE	**SETS × REPS (% 1RM OR INTENSITY)**
Abdominal work	3 × 20. Choose 3 exercises and superset them.
Light stretching	5 minutes
Dip	3 × to failure
Military press (SS)	3 × 8 (75 to 80%)
Dumbbell rear shoulder raise (SS)	3 × 8 (70 to 75%)
Dumbbell fly	3 × 8 (70 to 75%)
Dumbbell triceps extension	3 × 10 (75 to 80%)

Week 5 **Off-Season**

MONDAY

Resistance training

EXERCISE	SETS × REPS (% 1RM OR INTENSITY)
Abdominal work	Choose 4 exercises × 20 to 30.
Light stretching	5 minutes
Squat or leg press* (SS) (PW)	4 × 5 (65, 75, 80, 80%)
(SW)	4 × 5 (65, 70, 75, 75%)
Hip abduction (tubing) (SS)	3 × 8 each leg
Dumbbell leg curl	3 × 6 (85 to 90%)
Back extension	3 × 15 to 20
Heel raise	4 × 10 (80 to 85%)

* Squat or leg press: If at any time you are able to do the weight prescribed by the percentages while achieving all reps on every set, then go up 10 lb on your squat or leg press max on your next workout.

TUESDAY

Conditioning

Low-intensity aerobic activity for 35 to 45 minutes (65 to 70% max heart rate).

Stretch 10 minutes.

WEDNESDAY

Resistance training

EXERCISE	SETS × REPS (% 1RM OR INTENSITY)
Abdominal work	Choose 4 exercises × 20 to 30.
Light stretching	5 minutes
Bench press*(PW)	4 × 5 (65, 75, 80, 80%)
(SW)	4 × (65, 70, 75, 75%)
Dumbbell incline press)	3 × 5 (80 to 85%)
Push press* (PW)	4 × 5 (65, 75, 80, 80%)
(SW)	4 × 5 (65, 70, 75, 75%)
Dumbbell front shoulder raise	3 × 6 (75 to 80%)
Triceps cable push-down	3 × 10 to 15 (70 to 75%)

* Bench press and push press: If at any time you are able to do all the weight prescribed by the percentages while achieving all reps for every set, go up 5 lb on your bench press or push press max on your next workout.

THURSDAY

Conditioning

Low-intensity aerobic activity for 35 to 45 minutes (65 to 70% max heart rate).

Stretch 10 minutes.

Week 5 *(continued)*

FRIDAY	Resistance training	
	EXERCISE	**SETS × REPS (% 1RM or INTENSITY)**
	Abdominal work	Choose 4 exercises × 20 to 30.
	Light stretching	5 minutes
	Leg extension	3 × 10 to 12 (70 to 75%)
	Single-leg squat (SS)	3 × 5 (80 to 85%)
	Leg press (SS) (PW)	4 × 6 (65, 75, 80, 85%)
	(SW)	4 × 6 (65, 70, 75, 75%)
	Machine leg curl	3 × 6 (80 to 85%)
	Hang clean	3 × 5 (80 to 85%)
	Machine row	3 × 5 (80 to 85%)
	Reverse hyperextension	3 × 10 to 15
	Heel raise	4 × 10 (80 to 85%)

Week 6 Off-Season

MONDAY

Resistance training

EXERCISE	SETS × REPS (% 1RM OR INTENSITY)
Abdominal work	Choose 4 exercises × 20 to 30.
Light stretching	5 minutes
Bench press (PW)	4 × 5 (65, 75, 80, 80%)
(SW)	4 × 5 (65, 70, 75, 75%)
Dip	3 × to failure
Push press (PW)	4 × 5 (65, 75, 80, 80%)
(SW)	4 × 5 (65, 75, 75, 75%)
Dumbbell side raise	3 × 6 (80 to 85%)
Reverse triceps push-up (on bench)	3 × to failure

TUESDAY

Conditioning

Low-intensity aerobic activity for 35 to 45 minutes (65 to 70% max heart rate).

Stretch 10 minutes.

WEDNESDAY

Resistance training

EXERCISE	SETS × REPS (% 1RM OR INTENSITY)
Abdominal work	3 × circuit of 3 exercises of 15 to 30 reps (rest 30 seconds between sets)
Light stretching	5 minutes
Leg extension (SS)	3 × 10 to 12 (70 to 75%)
Single-leg squat (SS)	3 × 6 (75 to 80%)
Hip abduction (tubing) (SS)	3 × 10 each leg
Dumbbell leg curl (SS)	3 × 6 to 8 (85 to 90%)
Hang clean	3 × 5 (75 to 80%)
Lat pull-down	3 × 6 (75 to 80%)
Biceps curl	3 × 6 (75 to 80%)
Reverse hyperextension	3 × 15 to 20
Heel raise	4 × 10 (80 to 85%)

Week 6 *(continued)*

THURSDAY

Conditioning

Do the following in the shallow end of the pool (from side to side). Water should be waist high. You may also use an aqua vest during this workout.

Warm up with one lap of each of the following:

- Walk in the snow
- Heel-toe walk
- Russian march
- Butt kick
- Backward walk and reach
- Power skip
- High knee pump
- Carioca
- Tight S
- Power slide right – left

Workout:

- Double-leg bound across pool
- Vertical jump 1 × 8
- Single-leg vertical jump 3 × 6
- Sprint work 2 × 6
- Run in place with high knee pumps (for speed) 3 × 15 seconds

Cool down with a relaxing swim.

FRIDAY

Resistance training

EXERCISE	SETS × REPS (% 1RM OR INTENSITY)
Abdominal work	3 × circuit of 3 exercises of 15 to 20 reps (rest 30 seconds between sets)
Light stretching	5 minutes
Dumbbell incline press	3 × 5 (80 to 85%)
Push-up (SS)	3 × to failure
Close-grip bench press (SS)	3 × 6 (80 to 85%)
Dumbbell rear shoulder raise (Swiss ball)	3 × 6 to 8 (75 to 80%)
Triceps cable push-down (SS)	3 × 10 to 15 (70 to 75%)
Reverse triceps push-up (on bench) (SS)	3 × to failure

Week 7 **Off-Season**

MONDAY

Resistance training

EXERCISE	SETS × REPS (% 1RM OR INTENSITY)
Abdominal work	3 × circuit of 3 exercises of 15 to 30 reps (rest 30 seconds between sets)
Light stretching	5 minutes
Leg extension	3 × 10 to 12 (70 to 75%)
Box squat	4 × 5 to 6 (80 to 85%)
Walking lunge (SS)	2 × 20 to 30 yards
Machine leg curl (SS)	3 × 6 (80 to 85%)
Side step-up	3 × 6 (10- to 25-lb dumbbells)
Hang clean	3 × 5 (80 to 85%)
Chin-up	3 × to failure
Heel raise	4 × 10 (80 to 85%)
Back extension	3 × 15 to 20

TUESDAY

Conditioning

Jump rope for 150 to 200 contacts.

Low-intensity activity for 35 to 45 minutes (65 to 70% max heart rate).

Stretch 10 minutes.

WEDNESDAY

Resistance training

EXERCISE	SETS × REPS (% 1RM OR INTENSITY)
Abdominal work	3 × circuit of 3 exercises of 15 to 30 reps (rest 30 seconds between sets)
Light stretching	5 minutes
Dumbbell incline press	3 × 5 (80 to 85%)
Push press (SS) (PW)	3 × 5 (65, 75, 80%)
(SW)	3 × 5 (65, 70, 75%)
Dumbbell front shoulder raise (SS)	3 × 6 (80 to 85%)
Triceps cable push-down (SS)	3 × 10 to 15 (80 to 85%)
Close-grip bench press (SS)	3 × 5 (80 to 85%)

THURSDAY

Conditioning

Jump rope for 150 to 200 contacts.

Low-intensity activity for 35 to 45 minutes (65 to 70% max heart rate).

Stretch 10 minutes.

Week 7 *(continued)*

Resistance training	
EXERCISE	**SETS × REPS (% 1RM OR INTENSITY)**
Abdominal work	3 × circuit of 3 exercises of 15 to 30 reps (rest 30 seconds between sets)
Light stretching	5 minutes
Front squat or	4 × 6 (75 to 80%)
Leg press (PW)	4 × 6 (65, 75, 80, 80%)
(SW)	4 × 6 (65, 70, 75, 75%)
Side squat	3 × 6 each leg (75 to 80%)
Straight-leg deadlift	3 × 6 (75 to 80%)
Machine or cable row	3 × 6 (75 to 80%)
Reverse hyperextension	3 × 10 to 15
Heel raise	4 × 10 (75 to 80%)

(Row label: **FRIDAY**)

Week 8 **Off-Season**

Rest week

Off-Season Phase II

Phase II of the off-season is six weeks long, including one rest week. Because basketball is a game that relies on balance and stability, this phase emphasizes these two factors. A Swiss ball or a balance pad, which most gyms provide, figures more prominently in phase II. If you do not have a balance pad, simply stand on one leg. Chapter 7 offers a variety of Swiss ball and single-leg exercises for developing stability and balance.

Resistance Training

Phase II's resistance training switches from alternating the two different workouts each week to doing specific exercises on Mondays, Wednesdays, and Fridays. This program helps promote muscular strength and the freshness of major joints of the knees and ankles. Monday's and Friday's workouts focus on the chest, legs, hips, and biceps, and Wednesday's workout includes back, shoulder, and triceps exercises. Friday's workout also includes triceps work.

Phase II also includes complex movement lifts. These lifts are the summation of two or more multijoint exercises (e.g., the hang clean to the front squat) or other movements performed within one set. For example, say that your workout calls for you to do a hang clean and a front squat for 3×5. Normally you would do all sets of the hang clean, then all sets of the front squat, but with the combination movements, you perform five reps for the hang clean and then on your last rep you keep the bar across your upper chest and shoulders and go right into your front squat for five reps. Another way to perform a complex movement lift is to do one rep on the hang clean and then go right into the front squat for one rep, then repeat until you have five total reps. The choice is yours. Chapter 7 provides more information on complex movement lifts.

In this phase you also begin using another principle called *contrast training* during your resistance workouts (see also chapter 7). This requires going from an absolute strength exercise (squat) to an explosive exercise such as a dumbbell jump in a superset manner. It can involve upper body movements such as the bench press and medicine ball chest pass, or an explosive lift or movement first and then an absolute strength movement. It is fun to mix it up in the weight room because this is what trains you for the plays you encounter in a game.

Conditioning

Your conditioning workouts are still on Tuesdays and Thursdays; however, you switch from the treadmill, bike, or stepper to the outdoor running track at your local high school or college. You have already established a base by doing endurance conditioning work in the gym, but now it's time to put more stress on your cardiovascular system by upping the intensity of your conditioning workouts. During the first two weeks of this phase you will continue with your mile runs. Later in the phase, however, you will move to 800-meter runs (two laps around a standard outdoor track), which will train your aerobic system. (See chapter 1, pages 3 to 4 for information on these systems.)

Week 9 **Off-Season**

MONDAY

Resistance training

EXERCISE	SETS × REPS (% 1RM OR INTENSITY)
Abdominal work	3 × circuit of 3 exercises of 15 to 30 reps (rest 30 seconds between sets)
Light stretching	5 minutes
Rotator cuff work	Choose 1 exercise × 8 to 10 (pages 142 to 144).
Bench press * (SS) (PW)	3 × 10 (65, 70, 75%)
(SW)	3 × 10 (65, 70, 70%)
Medicine ball chest pass (SS)	3 × 10 throws
Leg extension	2 × 10 (75 to 80%)
Squat or leg press * (SS)	3 × 10 (65, 70, 75%)
Dumbbell jump (SS)	3 × 8 jumps (10- to 15-lb dumbbell)
Machine leg curl	3 × 10 (75 to 80%)
Triceps cable push-down	4 × 10 to 15 (75 to 80%)

* Bench, squat, or leg press: If at any time you are able to do the weight prescribed by the percentages while achieving all reps for every set, go up 5 lb on your bench press and 10 lb on your squat or leg press max.

TUESDAY

Conditioning

Running warm-ups (see chapter 1)

Light stretching for 5 minutes

Track work: Mile run at a 6:45 to 7:15 pace, walk 200 meters to cool down

Light stretching for 10 minutes

WEDNESDAY

Resistance training

EXERCISE	SETS × REPS (% 1RM OR INTENSITY)
Abdominal work	3 × circuit of 3 exercises of 15 to 30 reps (rest 30 seconds between sets)
Light stretching	5 minutes
Hang clean	3 × 8 (75 to 80%)
Push press (PW)	3 × 8 (65, 70, 75%)
(SW)	3 × 8 (65, 70, 70%)
Lat pull-down	3 × 8 (80 to 85%)
Dumbbell rear shoulder raise (Swiss ball)	3 × 8 (75 to 80%)
Biceps curl (SS)	3 × 8 (75 to 80%)
Dumbbell hammer curl (single-leg) (SS)	3 × 10 each leg (75 to 80%)
Good morning	3 × 10 (bar only)

THURSDAY

Conditioning

Running warm-ups (see chapter 1)

Light stretching for 5 minutes

Track work: Mile run at a 6:45 to 7:00 pace, walk 200 meters to cool down

Light stretching for 10 minutes

Week 9 *(continued)*

Resistance training	
EXERCISE	**SETS × REPS (% 1RM OR INTENSITY)**
Abdominal work	3 × circuit of 3 exercises of 15 to 30 reps (rest 30 seconds between sets)
Light stretching	5 minutes
Dumbbell bench press	3 × 10 (80 to 85%)
Basketball push-up	3 × to failure
Leg extension	2 × 10 to 12 (70 to 75%)
Front squat	3 × 10 (75 to 80%)
Machine leg curl (SS)	3 × 10 (75 to 80%)
Side lunge (SS)	2 × 10 (70 to 75%)
Biceps/triceps work (pick any exercise)	3 × 8 (75 to 80%)
Heel raise	4 × 10 (80 to 85%)

FRIDAY

Week 10 Off-Season

MONDAY

Resistance training

EXERCISE	SETS × REPS (% 1RM OR INTENSITY)
Abdominal work	3 × circuit of 3 exercises of 15 to 30 reps (rest 30 seconds between sets)
Light stretching	5 minutes
Rotator cuff work	Choose 1 exercise × 8 to 10.
Bench press (SS) (PW)	3 × 10 (65, 70, 70%)
(SW)	3 × 10 (65, 70, 75%)
Medicine ball chest pass (SS)	3 × 10 throws
Leg extension	2 × 10 (75 to 80%)
Squat or leg press (SS) (PW)	3 × 10 (65, 70, 75%)
(SW)	3 × 10 (65, 70, 70%)
Dumbbell jump (SS)	3 × 8 jumps (10- to 15-lb dumbbells)
Machine leg curl	3 × 10 (75 to 80%)
Reverse triceps push-up	3 × to failure

TUESDAY

Conditioning

Running warm-ups

Light stretching for 5 minutes

Track work: Mile run at a 6:30 to 7:00 pace, walk 200 meters to cool down

Light stretching for 10 minutes

WEDNESDAY

Resistance training

EXERCISE	SETS × REPS (% 1RM OR INTENSITY)
Abdominal work	3 × circuit of 3 exercises of 15 to 30 reps (rest 30 seconds between sets)
Light stretching	5 minutes
Hang clean	3 × 8 (75 to 80%)
Military press	3 × 8 (80 to 85%)
Machine or cable row	3 × 10 (80 to 85%)
Dumbbell side raise (standing, single-leg)	3 × 10 each leg (75 to 80%)
Biceps curl	3 × 10 (75 to 80%)
Reverse arm curl (standing, with bar)	3 × 10 (70 to 75%)
Reverse hyperextension (Swiss ball)	3 × 15 to 20

THURSDAY

Conditioning

Running warm-ups

Light stretching for 5 minutes

Track work: Mile run at a 6:30 to 6:45 pace, walk 200 meters to cool down

Light stretching for 10 minutes

Week 10   *(continued)*

FRIDAY

Resistance training	
EXERCISE	**SETS × REPS (% 1RM OR INTENSITY)**
Abdominal work	3 × circuit of 3 exercises of 15 to 30 reps (rest 30 seconds between sets)
Light stretching	5 minutes
Dumbbell incline press (SS)	3 × 8 (70 to 85%)
Swiss ball walkout push-up (SS)	3 × to failure
Leg extension	2 × 10 to 12 (70 to 75%)
Front squat	3 × 10 (75 to 80%)
Swiss ball leg curl	3 × 10
Crossover side step-up (SS)	3 × 6 each side (10- to 25-lb dumbbell)
Biceps/triceps work (pick any exercise)	3 × 8 (75 to 80%)
Heel raise	4 × 10 (75 to 80%)

Week 11 **Off-Season**

MONDAY

Resistance training

EXERCISE	SETS × REPS (% 1RM OR INTENSITY)
Abdominal work	3 × circuit of 3 exercises of 15 to 30 reps (rest 30 seconds between sets)
Light stretching	5 minutes
Rotator cuff work	Choose 1 exercise × 8 to 10.
Bench press * (SS) (PW)	4 × 6 (65, 75, 80, 85%)
(SW)	4 × 6 (65, 70, 75, 75%)
Medicine ball chest pass (SS)	4 × 6 throws
Leg extension	2 × 10 to 12 (75 to 80%)
Squat or leg press* (PW)	4 × 6 (65, 75, 80, 85%)
(SW)	4 × 6 (65, 70, 75, 75%)
Straight-leg deadlift	3 × 6 (80 to 85%)
Hip abductions (tubing)	3 × 6 each leg
Dumbbell hammer curl	3 × 8 (75 to 80%)
Heel raise	4 × 10 (75 to 80%)

* Bench press, squat, or leg press: If at any time you are able to do the weight prescribed by the percentages while achieving all reps for every set, go up 5 lb on your bench press and 10 lb on your squat or leg press max.

TUESDAY

Conditioning

Running warm-ups

Light stretching for 5 minutes

Track work: 2 × 800 meters at a 2:30 to 2:45 pace. Take a 2:30 rest between runs. Walk 200 meters after the second run to cool down.

Light stretching for 10 minutes

WEDNESDAY

Resistance training

EXERCISE	SETS × REPS (% 1RM OR INTENSITY)
Hang clean to front squat to push press	3 each × 6 (70 to 75%)
Chin-up (feet on Swiss ball) (CS)	3 × to failure
Single-leg dumbbell press (CS)	3 × 6 each leg (80 to 85%)
Triceps cable push-down	3 × 10 (75 to 80%)
Abdominal work	Choose 4 exercises × 15 to 30.

THURSDAY

Conditioning

Running warm-ups

Light stretching for 5 minutes

Track work: 2 × 800 meters at a 2:25 to 2:40 pace. Take a 2:30 rest between runs. Walk 200 meters after the second run to cool down.

Light stretching for 10 minutes

Week 11   *(continued)*

FRIDAY

Resistance training	
EXERCISE	**SETS × REPS (% 1RM OR INTENSITY)**
Abdominal work	3 × circuit of 3 exercises of 15 to 30 reps (rest 30 seconds between sets)
Light stretching	5 minutes
Floor bench press (SS)	3 × 6 (75 to 85%)
Basketball push-up (SS)	3 × failure
Leg extension	2 × 10 to 12 (75 to 80%)
Single-leg squat	3 × 6 (80 to 85%)
Romanian deadlift	3 × 6 (80 to 85%)
Heel raise	3 × 10 (80 to 85%)
Biceps/triceps work (pick any exercise)	3 × 6 to 10 (80 to 85%)

Week 12 Off-Season

MONDAY

Resistance training

EXERCISE	SETS × REPS (% 1RM OR INTENSITY)
Abdominal work	3 × circuit of 3 exercises of 15 to 30 reps (rest 30 seconds between sets)
Light stretching	5 minutes
Rotator cuff work	Choose 1 exercise × 8 to 10.
Bench press (PW)	4 × 5 (65, 75, 80, 80%)
(SW)	4 × 5 (65, 70, 75, 75%)
Dumbbell incline press (SS)	3 × 5 (75 to 85%)
Medicine ball chest pass (SS)	3 × 5 throws
Machine leg curl (CS)	3 × 6 (80 to 85%)
Leg extension (CS)	3 × 10 to 12 (75 to 80%)
Box squat (PW)	4 × 6 (65, 75, 80, 80%)
(SW)	4 × 6 (65, 75, 80, 80%)
Biceps curl	3 × 6 to 10 (80 to 85%)
Heel raise	4 × 10 (80 to 85%)

TUESDAY

Conditioning

Running warm-ups

Light stretching for 5 minutes

Track work: 800 meters at a 2:20 to 2:35 pace followed by a 2:25 rest. Then 600 meters at a 1:50 pace followed by a 200-meter walk.

Light stretching for 10 minutes

WEDNESDAY

Resistance training

EXERCISE	SETS × REPS (% 1RM OR INTENSITY)
Hang clean to front squat to push press	3 × 5 (75 to 80%)
Chin-up (CS)	3 × to failure
Dumbbell side raise (CS)	3 × 6 (75 to 80%)
Reverse triceps push-up	3 × to failure
Abdominal work	4 × 15 to 30

THURSDAY

Conditioning

Running warm-ups

Light stretching for 5 minutes

Track work: 800 meters at a 2:15 to 2:30 pace followed by a 2:25 rest. Then 600 meters at a 1:45 pace followed by a 200-meter walk.

Light stretching for 10 minutes

Week 12 *(continued)*

	Resistance training	
	EXERCISE	**SETS × REPS (% 1RM OR INTENSITY)**
FRIDAY	Abdominal work	3 × circuit of 3 exercises of 15 to 30 reps (rest 30 seconds between sets)
	Light stretching	5 minutes
	Dumbbell bench press (SS)	3 × 5 (75 to 85%)
	Dip (SS)	3 × to failure
	Leg extension	3 × 10 to 12 (75 to 80%)
	Single-leg squat	3 × 5 each leg (75 to 80%)
	Swiss ball leg curl	3 × 6
	Biceps/triceps work (pick any exercise)	3 × 6 to 10 (80 to 85%)
	Heel raise	4 × 10 (80 to 85%)

Week 13 Off-Season

MONDAY

Resistance training

EXERCISE	SETS × REPS (% 1RM OR INTENSITY)
Abdominal work	3 × circuit of 3 exercises of 15 to 30 reps (rest 30 seconds between sets)
Light stretching	5 minutes
Rotator cuff work	Choose 1 exercise × 8 to 11.
Bench press (PW)	4 × 5 (65, 75, 80, 85%)
(SW)	4 × 5 (65, 70, 75, 75%)
Dumbbell incline press (CS)	3 × 5 (75 to 85%)
Dumbbell pullover (CS)	3 × 6 (80 to 85%)
Leg extension	3 × 10 to 12 (75 to 80%)
Squat or leg press (PW)	4 × 5 (65, 75, 80, 85%)
(SW)	4 × 5 (65, 70, 75, 75%)
Side lunge	2 × 6 (75 to 80%)
Dumbbell hammer curl	3 × 6 to 10 (75 to 80%)
Heel raise	4 × 10 (80 to 85%)

TUESDAY

Conditioning

Running warm-ups

Light stretching for 5 minutes

Track work: 3 × 600 meters at a 1:45 pace with a 3:30 rest between runs. Follow set with a 200-meter walk.

Light stretching for 10 minutes

WEDNESDAY

Resistance training

EXERCISE	SETS × REPS (% 1RM OR INTENSITY)
Hang clean to front squat to push press	3 each × 5 (75 to 80%)
Lat pull-down (SS)	3 × 5 (80 to 85%)
Dumbbell front shoulder raise (single-leg) (SS)	3 × 6 (3 right, 3 left) (75 to 80%)
Dumbbell kickback	3 × 6 to 10 (75 to 80%)
Abdominal work	4 × 15 to 30

THURSDAY

Conditioning

Running warm-ups

Light stretching for 5 minutes

Track work: 3 × 600 meters at a 1:40 to 1:50 pace with a 3:20 rest between runs. Follow set with a 200-meter walk.

Light stretching for 10 minutes

Week 13 *(continued)*

Resistance training	
EXERCISE	**SETS × REPS (% 1RM OR INTENSITY)**
Abdominal work	3 × circuit of 3 exercises of 15 to 30 reps (rest 30 seconds between sets)
Light stretching	5 minutes
Dumbbell incline press	3 × 5 (75 to 85%)
Dumbbell fly	3 × 6 (75 to 80%)
Leg extension	3 × 10 to 12 (75 to 80%)
Machine leg curl (SS)	3 × 6 (80 to 85%)
Box squat (PW)	4 × 5 (65, 75, 80, 85%)
(SW)	4 × 5 (65, 70, 75, 75%)
Medicine ball jump	4 × 5 jumps
Biceps/triceps work (pick any exercise)	3 × 6 to 10 (75 to 80%)

FRIDAY

Week 14 **Off-Season**

Rest week

Off-Season Phase III

This phase lasts seven weeks and helps prepare you for the beginning of your preseason work, which is covered in chapter 3.

Resistance Training

In the seven weeks of phase III off-season workouts, you go back to alternating workouts as you did in phase I. During this phase you also begin your plyometric or jump program once or twice a week to help increase your explosiveness, which in turn leads to a higher vertical jump (see chapter 7 for more details on jump training exercises).

Conditioning

Your conditioning workouts are planned for Tuesdays and Thursdays and consist of short-duration, high-intensity anaerobic work on the track and baseball field. The high-intensity conditioning at this time prepares you for the preseason conditioning that centers on sport-specific skill work such as agility, footwork, and full-court basketball drills.

Skill Training

At this time I suggest that you *put up and make 100 shots* at least five to six times a week. If you are a center or forward, 80% of your shots should be low post shots and midrange jumpers. If you are a 1 or 2 guard, 80% should be midrange to outside jumpers and 20% should be in the paint. Do not forget your free throws; try to finish each session by shooting 30 to 50 free throws. Sometimes during this phase of training I throw in a free throw shooting game; however, you are free to play it anytime throughout this phase with your workout partner or friend. Play a 15-point game in which a rim shot scores 1 point, nothing but net is 2 points, and a miss is minus 1 point. Remember that any extra work, no matter how small, in a certain area of your game may pay big dividends down the road. What you work on now may help your team win a game four to six months from now.

Week 15 **Off-Season**

MONDAY

Resistance training

EXERCISE	SETS × REPS (% 1RM OR INTENSITY)
Dumbbell incline press	3 × 8 (75 to 80%)
Push press	3 × 8 (65, 70, 70%)
Dumbbell side raise (single-leg)	3 × 10 each leg (75 to 80%)
Triceps cable push-down	3 × 10 to 15 (70 to 75%)

TUESDAY

Conditioning

Running warm-ups

Light stretching for 5 minutes

Track work: 3 × 400 meters (one lap) at a 1:15 to 1:30 pace. Rest 2:30 between runs. Follow set with a 200-meter walk.

Light stretching for 10 minutes

WEDNESDAY

Resistance training

EXERCISE	SETS × REPS (% 1RM OR INTENSITY)
Abdominal work	3 × circuit of 3 exercises of 15 to 30 reps (rest 30 seconds between sets) (pages 131 to 135)
Light stretching	5 minutes
Leg extension	3 × 10 to 12 (75 to 80%)
Squat or leg press (SS)	4 × 10 (65, 70, 70, 70%)
Box jump-up (SS)	4 × 8 jumps (18- to 24-in. box height)
Bench step-up (single-leg)	3 × 10
Machine leg curl	3 × 10 (75 to 80%)
Hang clean (SS)	3 × 8 (75 to 80%)
Lat pull-down (SS)	3 × 8 (75 to 80%)
Dumbbell hammer curl	3 × 8 (75 to 80%)
Heel raise	4 × 10 (75 to 80%)

THURSDAY

Conditioning

Running warm-ups

Light stretching for 5 minutes

Track work: 3 × 400 meters (one lap) at a 1:15 to 1:30 pace. Rest 2:30 between runs. Follow set with a 200-meter walk.

Light stretching for 10 minutes

Week 15 *(continued)*

FRIDAY

Resistance training	
EXERCISE	**SETS × REPS (% 1RM OR INTENSITY)**
Abdominal work	3 × circuit of 3 exercises of 15 to 30 reps (rest 30 seconds between sets)
Light stretching	5 minutes
Floor bench press (SS)	3 × 10 (75 to 80%)
Medicine ball chest pass (SS)	3 × 10 throws
Close-grip bench press	3 × 8 (75 to 80%)
Basketball push-up (SS)	3 × to failure
Dumbbell front shoulder raise (SS)	3 × 8 (70 to 75%)

Skill training

Free throw shooting game. First one to 15 wins. Ball hits the rim and goes in = 1 point; nothing but net = 2 points; miss the shot = minus 1 point.

Week 16 **Off-Season**

MONDAY

Resistance training

EXERCISE	SETS × REPS (% 1RM OR INTENSITY)
Abdominal work	Choose 4 exercises × 15 to 30.
Light stretching	5 minutes
Leg extension	3 × 10 to 12 (75 to 80%)
Box squat (SS)	4 × 10 (65, 70, 70, 70%)
Repetitive quick jumps (SS)	4 × 10 jumps
Hang clean	3 × 8 (75 to 80%)
Machine leg curl (CS)	3 × 8 (75 to 80%)
Swiss ball chin-up (CS)	3 × failure
Dumbbell hammer curl (single-leg)	3 × 10 (5 right, 5 left) (75 to 80%)
Heel raise	4 × 10 (75 to 80%)

Skill training

Make 100 shots.

TUESDAY

Conditioning

Running warm-ups

Light stretching for 5 minutes

Track work: 3 × 400 meters (one lap) at a 1:15 to 1:25 pace. Rest 2:30 between runs. Follow set with a 200-meter walk.

Light stretching for 10 minutes

Skill training

Make 100 shots.

WEDNESDAY

Resistance training

EXERCISE	SETS × REPS (% 1RM OR INTENSITY)
Abdominal work	3 × circuit of 3 exercises of 15 to 30 reps (rest 30 seconds between sets)
Light stretching	5 minutes
Rotator cuff work	Choose 1 exercise × 8 to 10 (pages 142 to 144).
Dumbbell incline press (CS)	3 × 8 (75 to 80%)
Dumbbell side raise (single-leg) (CS)	3 × 8 each leg (75 to 80%)
Dumbbell kickback	3 × 10 (75 to 80%)

Skill training

Make 100 shots.

THURSDAY

Conditioning

Running warm-ups

Light stretching for 5 minutes

Track work: 3 × 400 meters at a 1:10 to 1:20 pace. Rest 2:30 between runs. Follow set with a 200-meter walk.

Light stretching for 10 minutes

Skill training

Make 100 shots.

FRIDAY

Resistance training

EXERCISE	SETS × REPS (% 1RM OR INTENSITY)
Abdominal work	Choose 4 exercises × 15 to 30
Light stretching	5 minutes
Leg extension	3 × 10 to 12 (75 to 80%)
Single-leg squat (SS)	4 × 8 (75 to 80%)
Single-leg vertical jump (SS)	4 × 8 with each leg
Lat pull-down (SS)	4 × 8 (75 to 80%)
Romanian deadlift (SS)	4 × 8 (75 to 80%)
Biceps curl	4 × 8 to 10 (75 to 80%)
Heel raise	4 × 10 (75 to 80%)

Skill training

Free throw shooting game. First one to 15 wins. Ball hits the rim and goes in = 1 point; nothing but net = 2 points; miss the shot = minus 1 point.

Make 100 shots.

Week 17 **Off-Season**

Resistance training

EXERCISE	SETS × REPS (% 1RM OR INTENSITY)
Abdominal work	3 × circuit of 3 exercises of 15 to 30 reps (rest 30 seconds between sets)
Light stretching	5 minutes
Rotator cuff work	Choose 1 exercise × 8 to 10.
Bench press (PW)	4 × 5 (65, 75, 80, 85%)
(SW)	4 × 5 (65, 70, 70, 75%)
Medicine ball chest pass	3 × 10 to 12 throws
Dip (PW)	3 × 5 to 8 (weighted)
(SW)	3 × 5 to failure (no weight)
Push press (SS) (PW)	3 × 5 (65, 75, 85%)
(SW)	3 × 5 (65, 70, 70%)
Dumbbell rear shoulder raise (Swiss ball) (SS)	3 × 6 (75 to 80%)
Triceps cable push-down	3 × 10 to 12 (75 to 80%)

MONDAY

Skill training

Make 100 shots.

Conditioning

Running warm-ups followed by light stretching for 5 minutes

Baseball field conditioning:

From foul pole to foul pole, the grass along the warning track is around 200 yards.

• Half pole: Run from one foul pole to center field in 12 to 15 seconds; walk to the other pole.

• Run from one pole to the other × 6 in 35 seconds. Rest 1:10 between runs.

• Walk to one foul pole for cool-down.

Light stretching for 10 minutes

TUESDAY

Skill training

Make 100 shots.

Resistance training

EXERCISE	SETS × REPS (% 1RM OR INTENSITY)
Abdominal work	Choose 4 exercises × 15 to 30.
Light stretching	5 minutes
Leg extension	3 × 10 to 12 (75 to 80%)
Squat or leg press (PW)	4 × 5 (65, 75, 80, 85%)
(SW)	4 × 5 (65, 70, 70, 75%)
Box jump-up (CS)	4 × 5 jumps (18- to 24-in. box height)
Side lunge (CS)	3 × 6 (80 to 85%)
Dumbbell leg curl (SS)	3 × 6 (80 to 85%)
Hang clean (SS)	3 × 5 (80 to 85%)
Lat pull-down (CS)	3 × 6 (80 to 85%)
Biceps curl (CS)	4 × 6 to 8 (75 to 80%)
Heel raise	4 × 10 to 12 (75 to 80%)
Reverse hyperextension	3 × 15 to 20

WEDNESDAY

WEDNESDAY

Skill training

Make 100 shots.

THURSDAY

Conditioning

Running warm-ups followed by light stretching for 5 minutes

Baseball field conditioning:

• Half pole: Run from one foul pole to center field in 12 to 15 seconds; walk to the other pole.

• Run from one pole to the other × 6 in 35 seconds. Rest 1:10 between runs.

• Walk to one foul pole for cool-down.

Light stretching for 10 minutes

Skill training

Make 100 shots.

FRIDAY

Resistance training

EXERCISE	SETS × REPS (% 1RM OR INTENSITY)
Abdominal work	3 × circuit of 3 exercises of 15 to 30 reps (rest 30 seconds between sets)
Light stretching for 5 minutes	5 minutes
Dumbbell incline press	3 × 5 (80 to 85%)
Close-grip bench press (SS)	3 × 5 (80 to 85%)
Military press (CS)	3 × 5 (80 to 85%)
Medicine ball chest pass (CS)	3 × 5 throws
Triceps cable push-down (SS)	3 × 10 to 15 (75 to 80%)
Reverse triceps push-up (SS)	3 × to failure

Skill training

Make 100 shots.

Week 18 Off-Season

MONDAY

Resistance training

EXERCISE	SETS × REPS (% 1RM OR INTENSITY)
Abdominal work	Choose 4 exercises × 15 to 30.
Light stretching	5 minutes
Leg extension	3 × 10 to 12 (75 to 80%)
Single-leg squat (SS)	3 × 6 (70 to 85%)
Box jump-up (single-leg) (SS)	3 × 6 jumps (12-in. box height)
Dumbbell split jump	10 jumps (70 to 75%)
Machine leg curl	4 × 6 (80 to 85%)
Hang clean	3 × 5 (80 to 85%)
Swiss ball chin-up	3 × to failure
Dumbbell hammer curl (single-leg)	3 × 10 (5 right, 5 left) (80 to 85%)
Reverse hyperextension (Swiss ball)	3 × 15 to 20
Heel raise	4 × 10 (80 to 85%)

Skill training

Make 100 shots.

TUESDAY

Conditioning

Running warm-ups followed by light stretching for 5 minutes

Baseball field conditioning
- Run half pole in 12 to 15 seconds (from pole to center field); then walk to the other foul pole.
- Run 2 poles in 65 seconds. Rest 2 minutes.
- Run 4 × 1 pole in 30 seconds. Rest 1 minute between runs.
- Walk 1 pole for cool-down.

Skill training

Make 100 shots.

WEDNESDAY

Resistance training

EXERCISE	SETS × REPS (% 1RM OR INTENSITY)
Abdominal work	3 × circuit of 3 exercises of 15 to 30 reps (rest 30 seconds between sets)
Light stretching	5 minutes
Rotator cuff work	Choose 1 exercise × 8 to 10.
Floor bench press (PW)	4 × 5 (65, 75, 80, 85%)
(SW)	4 × 5 (65, 70, 70, 75%)
Dip (PW)	3 × 6 to 8 (weighted)
(SW)	3 × to failure (no weight)
Push press (SS)	3 × 5 (65, 75, 85%)
Dumbbell side raise (single-leg) (SS)	3 × 5 (75 to 80%)
Dumbbell triceps extension (SS)	3 × 6 (80 to 85%)
Triceps cable push-down (SS)	3 × 10 to 12 (75 to 80%)

Week 18 *(continued)*

WEDNESDAY

Skill training

Make 100 shots.

THURSDAY

Conditioning

Running warm-ups followed by light stretching for 5 minutes

Baseball field conditioning
- Run half pole in 12 to 15 seconds (from pole to center field); then walk to the other foul pole.
- Run 2 poles in 65 seconds. Rest 2 minutes.
- Run 4 × 1 pole in 30 seconds. Rest 1 minute between runs.
- Walk 1 pole for cool-down.

Skill training

Make 100 shots.

FRIDAY

Resistance training

EXERCISE	SETS × REPS (% 1RM OR INTENSITY)
Abdominal work	Choose 4 exercises × 15 to 30.
Light stretching	5 minutes
Leg extension	3 × 10 (75 to 80%)
Front squat (CS)	3 × 6 (75 to 85%)
Dumbbell jump (CS)	3 × 6 jumps (10-to 15-lb dumbbells)
Crossover side step-up (CS)	3 × 6 (10- to 20-lb dumbbells)
Machine leg curl (CS)	3 × 6 (80 to 85%)
Dumbbell split jump	10 jumps (70 to 75%)
Machine or cable row (CS)	4 × 6 (80 to 85%)
Dumbbell hammer curl (CS)	4 × 6 to 8 (75 to 80%)
Back extension	3 × 15 to 20
Heel raise	4 × 10 (80 to 85%)

Skill training

Free throw shooting game. First one to 15 wins. Ball hits the rim and goes in = 1 point; nothing but net = 2 points; miss the shot = minus 1 point.

Make 100 shots.

Week 19 **Off-Season**

MONDAY

Resistance training

EXERCISE	SETS × REPS (% 1RM OR INTENSITY)
Abdominal work	3 × circuit of 3 exercises of 15 to 30 reps (rest 30 seconds between sets.
Light stretching	5 minutes
Rotator cuff work	Choose 1 exercise × 8 to 10.
Bench press (PW)	4 × 3 (70, 85, 87, 90%)
(SW)	4 × 3 (65, 70, 75, 75%)
Dumbbell fly	3 × 6 (80 to 85%)
Basketball push-up (SS)	3 × to failure
Close-grip bench press (SS)	3 × 3 (85 to 90%)
Dumbbell seated press	3 × 3 (85 to 90%)
Triceps cable push-down	3 × 8 to 10 (80 to 85%)

Skill training

Make 100 shots.

TUESDAY

Conditioning

Running warm-ups followed by light stretching for 5 minutes

Track work: 3 × 200 meters in 35 seconds (sprint). Rest 1:45 after each run. Then sprint 100 meters in 15 seconds. Walk 200 meters for cool-down.

Light stretching

Skill training

Make 100 shots.

WEDNESDAY

Resistance training

EXERCISE	SETS × REPS (% 1RM OR INTENSITY)
Abdominal work	Choose 4 exercises × 15 to 30.
Light stretching	5 minutes
Leg extension	3 × 10 to 12 (75 to 80%)
Squat or leg press (PW)	4 × 3 (70, 85, 87, 90%)
(SW)	4 × 3 (65, 70, 75, 75%)
Side lunge	3 × 5 (75 to 80%)
Box jump-up (single-leg) (SS)	3 × 5 jumps (12-in. box height)
Dumbbell split jump (SS)	10 jumps (70 to 75%)
Hang clean	3 × 3 (80 to 85%)
Chin-up (PW)	3 × 3 to 5 (weighted)
(SW)	3 × to failure
Romanian deadlift	3 × 5 (80 to 85%)
Dumbbell hammer curl (seated)	3 × 5 to 6 (80 to 85%)
Heel raise	4 × 10 (85 to 90%)

Skill training

Make 100 shots.

Week 19   *(continued)*

THURSDAY

Conditioning

Running warm-ups

Light stretching for 5 minutes

Track work: 3 × 200 meters in 35 seconds (sprint). Rest 1:30 after each run. Then sprint 100 meters in 15 seconds. Walk 200 meters for cool-down.

Light stretching for 10 minutes

Skill training

Make 100 shots.

FRIDAY

Resistance training

EXERCISE	SETS × REPS (% 1RM OR INTENSITY)
Abdominal work	3 × circuit of 3 exercises of 15 to 30 reps (rest 30 seconds between sets)
Light stretching	5 minutes
Dumbbell incline press (PW)	3 × 3 (85 to 90%)
(SW)	3 × 3 (75 to 80%)
Medicine ball pullover and throw (CS)	3 × 6 (12- to 20-lb medicine ball)
Push press (CS) (PW)	3 × 3 (85 to 90%)
(SW)	3 × 3 (75 to 80%)
Dumbbell side raise (single-leg)	3 × 6 each leg (75 to 80%)
Medicine ball side raise	3 × 10 (8- to 12-lb medicine ball)
Dumbbell triceps extension	3 × 5 (75 to 80%)

Skill training

Make 100 shots.

Week 20 **Off-Season**

MONDAY

Resistance training

EXERCISE	SETS × REPS (% 1RM OR INTENSITY)
Abdominal work	Choose 4 exercises × 15 to 20.
Light stretching	5 minutes
Leg extension	3 × 10 (75 to 80%)
Box squat (SS) (PW)	4 × 3 (70, 85, 87, 90%)
(SW)	4 × 3 (65, 70, 75, 75%)
Power slide	4 × 4 to 5 slides each side using just the bar (45 lb)
Machine leg curl	3 × 3 to 5 (85 to 90%)
Dumbbell split jump	10 jumps (70 to 75%)
Hang clean	3 × 3 (80 to 85%)
Swiss ball lat pull-down (single-arm)	3 × 3 to 5 (80 to 85%)
Biceps curl	3 × 3 to 6 (80 to 85%)
Good morning	3 × 5 to 6 (75 to 80%)
Heel raise	4 × 10 (80 to 85%)

Skill training

Make 100 shots.

TUESDAY

Conditioning

Running warm-ups followed by light stretching for 5 minutes

Track work (sprints):
- 2 × 200 meters in 30 seconds with a 1:30 rest after each
- 3 × 100 meters in 15 seconds with a 45-second rest after each
- 2 × 50 meters in 7 seconds with a 20-second rest after each
- 2 × 30 meters in 4 seconds with a 12-second rest after each
- Walk 200 meters for cool-down.

Light stretching for 10 minutes

Skill training

Make 100 shots.

WEDNESDAY

Resistance training

EXERCISE	SETS × REPS (% 1RM OR INTENSITY)
Light stretching	5 minutes
Rotator cuff work	Choose 1 exercise × 8 to 10.
Bench press (PW)	4 × 3 (70, 85, 87, 90%)
(SW)	4 × 3 (65, 70, 75, 80%)
Dip (PW)	3 × 6 (weighted)
(SW)	3 × to failure
Push press (PW)	3 × 3 (70, 85, 90%)
(SW)	3 × 3 (65, 70, 75%)
Dumbbell rear shoulder raise (CS)	3 × 5 to 6 (75 to 80%)
Reverse triceps push-up (CS)	3 × to failure
Medicine ball sit-up throw	3 × 15 to 30 (8- to 12-lb. ball) or 1 × to failure

WEDNESDAY

Skill training

Make 100 shots.

THURSDAY

Conditioning

Running warm-ups

Light stretching

Track work (sprints):

- 2 × 200 meters in 30 seconds with a 1:30 rest after each
- 3 × 100 meters in 15 seconds with a 45-second rest after each
- 2 × 50 meters in 7 seconds with a 20-second rest after each
- 2 × 30 meters in 4 seconds with a 12-second rest after each
- Walk 200 meters for cool-down.

Light stretching

Skill training

Make 100 shots.

FRIDAY

Resistance training

EXERCISE	SETS × REPS (% 1RM OR INTENSITY)
Abdominal work	Choose 4 exercises × 15 to 20.
Light stretching	5 minutes
Leg extension	3 × 10 (75 to 80%)
Front squat	3 × 3 (85 to 90%)
Box jump-up (SS)	3 × 5 jumps (18- to 24-in. box height)
Dumbbell split jump (SS)	10 jumps (70 to 75%)
Walking lunge	2 × 30 yards (use 45 lb to 99 lb)
Lat pull-down (PW)	3 × 3 to 5 (85 to 90%)
(SW)	3 × 3 to 5 (70 to 80%)
Medicine ball pullover and throw (CS)	3 × 5 (12- to 20-lb medicine ball)
Dumbbell hammer curl (single-leg) (SS)	3 × 3 each leg (85 to 90%)
Reverse hyperextension	3 × 10 to 15

Skill training

Free throw shooting game. First one to 15 wins. Ball hits the rim and goes in = 1 point; nothing but net = 2 points; miss the shot = minus 1 point.

Make 100 shots.

Week 21   **Off-Season**

MONDAY OR TUESDAY	**Testing**
	See chapter 1, pages 12 to 15 for procedures.
	Height with and without shoes
	Weight and body fat percentage
	Bench press
	Push press
	Squat or leg press

WEDNESDAY OR THURSDAY	**Testing**
	See chapter 1, pages 12 to 15 for procedures.
	Sit and reach
	Vertical jump
	20-yard shuttle
	300-yard shuttle

Preparing to Play: Preseason Workouts

The two preseason workout phases make up eight weeks of training. Phase I includes six weeks of all the tools to help you achieve maximum levels of performance—court sprint work, agility work, footwork, ball-handling drills, and shooting drills along with your resistance work and plyometrics. Phase II of your preseason program generally lasts about two weeks (the time between your first practice and your first regular season game) and includes many of the conditioning drills used in phase I. The goal of the preseason training weeks is to prepare you for the highest level of performance possible when it comes time to play the game.

Preseason Phase I

During phase I of your preseason program the volume (that is, the amount) of exercises in each workout is cut back. This is because you have already laid the foundation during your 21 weeks of off-season training. Now it is time to increase the skill work to help prepare you for your regular season. Your resistance work will remain on Mondays, Wednesdays, and Fridays and will be followed by ball-handling drills, agility work, and then your 100 to 150 shots. Your conditioning work will also remain on Tuesdays and Thursdays with an added short Saturday session of uphill sprints and optional ball-handling and shot work. The conditioning workouts on Tuesdays and Thursdays are also followed by ball-handling drills and resistance tubing work. A resistance tubing program will help you increase your vertical jump (explosiveness) and speed. Table 3.1 provides an overview of a typical training week during the preseason phase I.

Table 3.1 Typical Preseason Training Week

Monday	Tuesday	Wednesday	Thursday	Friday	Saturday
Weight training	Conditioning	Weight training	Conditioning	Weight training	Uphill sprints
Ball handling	Ball handling	Ball handling	Ball handling	Ball handling	Ball handling
Agility drills	Tubing/ medicine ball	Agility drills	Tubing/ medicine ball	Agility drills	Full-court pickup games
100 shots made	100 shots made	100 shots made	100 shots made	100 shots made	

Take Sundays off and play full court pickup games whenever possible.

Resistance Training and Plyometrics

The volume (sets and reps) of your resistance training over the six weeks of phase I of the preseason program is designed to ensure maximum strength gains and still enable you to decide which strength load you need for your body type. Power work (PW) is for athletes looking to maximize power and strength, whereas speed work (SW) is for those who do not need as much strength and mass but still want to increase speed and explosiveness.

Because you need more basketball skill work at this time, phase I preseason workouts call for a reduction in the number of exercises, or the volume, of your resistance training. Reducing the number of exercises keeps you from overtraining or burning out before your first day of practice. This is not to say that the intensity of your workouts drops off. The shorter period of weight training during the preseason gives you more energy for the skill work and conditioning to follow. Recovery during this time is of the utmost importance to help you get the most out of resistance training, conditioning, and drills.

Plyometric work is combined with weight training in this phase to link strength and explosiveness and to give you more time for agility and conditioning drills. Some plyometric jumps are also included with your agility work to add some intensity and variety to this type of training.

Note that some sets are to be done as supersets (two exercises that work the same body part with no rest between). These are marked as SS.

Conditioning

The preseason's main conditioning work is done on Tuesdays and Thursdays, with a short workout added on Saturdays. During the preseason, you are really getting some type of sport-specific conditioning each day with the addition of agility work and full-court pickup games whenever possible. I have included 20 conditioning drills to help you come into training camp (the first two weeks of official practice, see pages 77 to 78) in the best shape possible. Some of these drills are for conditioning purposes only, and some combine both conditioning and shooting drills. Specific drills are listed each conditioning day, or you may choose certain drills that you need extra work in. Just remember to work hard and have fun. The drills challenge you to become better and offer you the added benefit of knowing that you will be one of the most well-conditioned players reporting for the first day of practice! Chapter 8 provides a full description of each conditioning drill.

Skill Training

Skill training during the preseason consists of ball-handling drills, agility and footwork drills, medicine ball work, and resistance tubing work.

Ball Handling

Ball-handling drills should now be a part of your daily program. If you cannot control the basketball and make it do what you want it to do, then you will have a hard time controlling the game. Chapter 8 details several different ball-handling drills. I recommend that you select a different one each day or combine different drills in one session. Ball-handling work should last around 10 minutes. It is a great warm-up and should precede stretching, agility work, and all conditioning work.

Skill training gives you the confidence to take the ball to the basket.

Agility and Footwork

You can do agility and footwork drills right after weight training on Mondays, Wednesdays, and Fridays. I have planned the workouts so that some of your footwork drills are supersets or are combined with your weight training program. This way they also act as a short but intense conditioning tool. You have 17 different agility and footwork drills to choose from. Particular drills are listed on Mondays, Wednesdays, and Fridays; but you may choose one or two that fit your needs and goals more directly. See chapter 9 for details on how to perform each drill.

Medicine Ball Work

Of the hundreds of medicine ball drills, I have chosen seven that I think have fundamental applications to the game of basketball. Four can be used in the weight room, and three should be done on the court (see chapter 7). These drills will fit nicely into your program and make it well rounded and more complete. The medicine ball exercises done on the court with the resistance tubing will give you that increased explosiveness that is so important in the game.

Resistance Tubing

Coaches and players alike are always looking for that little something extra to help improve athletic performance. They may want to increase the vertical jump as much as possible or decrease the 40-yard dash time. Over the years I have found that working with resistance tubing to increase speed, explosiveness, and lateral movement has always given athletes that extra push to help them reach their individual goals. I recommend purchasing resistance surgical tubing or Thera-Bands to help you accomplish your goals. I like cutting Thera-Bands or any other tubing into 1.5- to 2-foot lengths and tying the ends together. That's usually big enough to fit both feet through.

Resistance tubing work takes place on Tuesdays and Thursdays after your regular conditioning work. You will really be able to tell the difference. I have included three types of work with the tubing—one for lateral speed, the next for vertical explosiveness, and the third for running speed. See chapter 7 for an explanation of each drill, as well as for information on a company to call in case you decide to purchase this type of equipment. I think you will find it most affordable and worth the price.

Saturday Preseason Workouts

As I have mentioned, you will have a Saturday conditioning day consisting of 40- to 60- yard uphill sprints followed by some optional ball-handling drills and your 100 shots. The uphill sprints are great for increasing speed, explosiveness, and muscular endurance. It is a very short workout, but it's very intense!

Week 22 **Preseason**

MONDAY

Resistance training

EXERCISE	SETS × REPS (% 1RM OR INTENSITY)
Abdominal work	3 × circuit of 3 exercises of 15 to 30 reps (rest 30 seconds between sets) (pages 131 to 135)
Light stretching	5 minutes
Rotator cuff work	Choose 1 exercise × 8 to 10 (pages 142 to 144).
Bench press* (SS)	4 × 10 (65, 70, 75, 75%)
Basketball push-up (SS)	4 × to failure
Leg extension	2 × 10 (70 to 75%)
Squat or leg press* (SS)	4 × 10 (65, 70, 75, 75%)
Dumbbell split jump (SS)	4 × 8 jumps (10- to 25-lb dumbbells)
Machine leg curl	3 × 10 (75 to 80%)
Triceps cable push-down	3 × 10 (75 to 80%)

* Remember to go up 5 lb on the bench press and 10 lb on the squat or leg press if you achieve all reps of every set.

Skill and agility training

Ball-handling drills for 10 minutes (see chapter 9 for drills)

Light stretching for 5 minutes

3 × 20 seconds of home base drill (see chapter 8). Rest 40 seconds between sets.

Jump rope routine

Make 100 shots.

TUESDAY

Conditioning and skill training

Running warm-ups (see chapter 1) followed by light stretching for 5 minutes

Ball-handling drills for 10 minutes

3 × ladder sprint (see chapter 8). Rest 1:30 between sets.

12 to 16 × medicine ball wall throw (see chapter 7). Rest 15 seconds between throws.

Make 100 shots.

WEDNESDAY

Resistance training

EXERCISE	SETS × REPS (% 1RM OR INTENSITY)
Light stretching	5 minutes
Hang clean	3 × 8 (75 to 80%)
Front squat	3 × 5 (65, 70, 75%)
Push press	3 × 5 (65, 70, 75%)
Lat pull-down (SS)	3 × 10 (75 to 80%)
Single-arm pullover (SS)	3 × 8
Biceps curl	3 × 8 to 10 (75 to 80%)
Dumbbell hammer curl (single-leg on Airex pad)	3 × 8 each leg (75 to 80%)
Heel raise	4 × 10 (75 to 80%)
Reverse hyperextension	3 × 10 to 15

Week 22   *(continued)*

WEDNESDAY

Skill and agility training

Ball-handling drills for 10 minutes

Light stretching for 5 minutes

Jump rope routine

3 × lateral box jump (20 seconds each) (see chapter 7). Rest 40 seconds between sets.

Make 100 shots.

THURSDAY

Conditioning and skill training

Running warm-ups followed by light stretching for 5 minutes

Ball-handling drills for 10 minutes

2 × 4, 8, 16 drill (see chapter 8). Rest 3 minutes between sets.

Make 100 shots.

15-point free throw game

FRIDAY

Resistance training

EXERCISE	SETS × REPS (% 1RM OR INTENSITY)
Abdominal work	4 × 15 to 30
Light stretching	5 minutes
Dumbbell incline press (Swiss ball) (SS)	3 × 10 (75 to 80%)
Medicine ball chest pass (SS)	3 × 10 (10- to 15-lb medicine ball)
Dip	3 × to failure
Leg extension	2 × 10 (70 to 75%)
Side lunge (SS)	3 × 8 (75 to 80%)
Body blade* (SS)	3 × 15 seconds each leg
Biceps curl	3 × 10 (75 to 80%)
Reverse triceps push-up	3 × to failure

* If body blade is not available, perform crossover side step-up (3 × 8 on each leg). See chapter 7 for both exercises.

Skill and agility training

Ball-handling drills for 10 minutes followed by light stretching for 5 minutes

Jump rope routine

4 × lane agility box drill (see chapter 9). Rest 15 seconds between sets.

3 × dot drill (see chapter 9)

Make 100 shots.

SATURDAY

Conditioning and skill training

Running warm-ups followed by light stretching for 5 minutes

8 × uphill sprint (see chapter 8). Walk back down the hill for rest time.

Ball-handling drills for 10 minutes

Make 100 shots (optional).

15-point free throw game

Full-court pickup game

Week 23 **Preseason**

MONDAY

Resistance training

EXERCISE	SETS × REPS (% 1RM OR INTENSITY)
Abdominal work	3 × circuit of 3 exercises of 15 to 30 reps (30 seconds rest between sets)
Light stretching	5 minutes
Rotator cuff work	Choose 1 exercise × 8 to 10.
Bench press (SS)	4 × 10 (65, 70, 75, 75%)
Swiss ball walkout push-up (SS)	4 × to failure
Leg extension	2 × 10 (70 to 75%)
Box squat	4 × 10 (65, 70, 75, 75%)
Dumbbell jump (SS)	4 × 8 jumps
Dumbbell leg curl (SS)	3 × 10 (80 to 85%)
Heel raise	3 × 10 (80 to 85%)
Dumbbell triceps extension	3 × 10 to 12 (70 to 75%)

Skill and agility training

Ball handling drills for 10 minutes followed by light stretching for 5 minutes

3 × dot drill. Rest 45 to 60 seconds between sets.

3 × star agility drill (see chapter 9). Rest 45 seconds between sets.

Make 100 shots.

TUESDAY

Conditioning and skill training

Running warm-ups followed by light stretching for 5 minutes

Ball-handling drills for 10 minutes

2 to 3 × sidewinder drill (see chapter 7). Rest 30 seconds between sets.

10 × 5 rim touch drill (see chapter 8)

1 × 10 to 14 medicine ball wall throw

Make 100 shots.

WEDNESDAY

Resistance training

EXERCISE	SETS × REPS (% 1RM OR INTENSITY)
Light stretching	10 minutes
Hang clean	3 × 8 (75 to 80%)
Front squat	3 × 5 (70, 75, 80%)
Push press	3 × 5 (70, 75, 80%)
Swiss ball floor press	2 × to failure
Swiss ball chin-up	3 × to failure
Medicine ball hold on Swiss ball	3 × 4 to 5 seconds
Biceps curl	3 × 8 to 10 (75 to 80%)
Heel raise	4 × 10 (80 to 85%)
Good morning	3 × 8 to 10 (70 to 75%)

Week 23 *(continued)*

WEDNESDAY

Skill and agility training

Ball-handling drills for 10 minutes followed by light stretching for 5 minutes

2 × dot drill. Rest 30 seconds between sets.

4 × pattern run (I or II) (see chapter 9). Rest 45 seconds between sets.

10 × wall quick feet (see chapter 7). Rest 3 to 5 seconds only.

Make 100 shots.

THURSDAY

Conditioning and skill training

Running warm-ups followed by light stretching for 5 minutes

Ball-handling drills for 10 minutes

6 × 30 second gassers (see chapter 8) with 90 seconds rest between sprints

10 to 12 × medicine ball squat throw (see chapter 7). Rest 30 seconds between throws.

Make 100 shots.

15-point free throw game

FRIDAY

Resistance training

EXERCISE	SETS × REPS (% 1RM OR INTENSITY)
Abdominal work	4 × 15 to 30
Light stretching	10 minutes
Floor bench press (SS)	3 × 10 (65, 70, 75%)
Medicine ball pullover and throw (SS)	3 × 8 (10- to 15-lb medicine ball)
Leg extension	2 × 10 (70 to 75%)
Single-leg squat (SS)	3 × 8 (75 to 80%)
Dumbbell split jump (SS)	4 × 8 jumps (10- to 25-lb dumbbells)
Body blade*	3 × 15 seconds each leg
Dumbbell hammer curl (single-leg on Airex pad)	3 × 10 each leg (75 to 80%)
Triceps cable push-down	3 × 10 to 12 (75 to 80%)

* Can do a dumbbell squat thrust and jump (10- to 15-lb dumbbell) instead of body blade.

Skill and agility training

Ball-handling drills for 10 minutes followed by light stretching for 5 minutes

3 × dot drill. Rest 45 to 60 seconds between sets.

4 × quick feet box step (15 seconds each) (see chapter 9). Rest 45 seconds between sets.

3 × dot drill. Rest 45 to 60 seconds between sets.

3 × triangle slide (see chapter 9). Rest 45 seconds between sets.

Make 100 shots.

SATURDAY

Conditioning and skill training

Running warm-ups followed by light stretching for 5 minutes

8 × uphill sprint. Walk back down the hill for rest.

Ball-handling drills for 10 minutes

Make 100 shots (optional).

15-point free throw game

Full-court pickup game

Week 24 **Preseason**

MONDAY

Resistance training	
EXERCISE	**SETS × REPS (% 1RM OR INTENSITY)**
Abdominal work	3 × circuit of 3 exercises of 15 to 30 reps (30 seconds rest between sets)
Light stretching	5 minutes
Rotator cuff work	Choose 1 exercise × 8 to 10
Bench press (PW)	4 × 5 (65, 75, 80, 85%)
(SW)	4 × 5 (65, 70, 75, 75%)
Dip (PW)	3 × 5 to 6 (weighted)
(SW)	3 × to failure (no weight)
Leg extension	2 × 10 (70 to 75%)
Leg press (PW)	3 × 5 to 6 (65, 75, 85%)
(SW)	3 × 5 to 6 (65, 75, 75%)
Dumbbell squat thrust and jump	3 × 5 to 6 (10- to 15-lb dumbbells)
Swiss ball leg curl (SS)	4 × 6
Heel raise (SS)	4 × 10 (80 to 85%)
Dumbbell kickback	3 × 10 (75 to 80%)

Skill and agility training

Ball handling drills for 10 minutes

Light stretching for 5 minutes

Jump rope routine

3 × cone or minihurdle jump (see chapter 9) (10 to 15 seconds each). Rest 10 to 15 seconds between sets.

5 × lane slide (see chapter 9). Rest 30 seconds between sets.

Make 100 shots.

TUESDAY

Conditioning and skill training

Running warm-ups

Light stretching for 5 minutes

Ball-handling drills for 10 minutes

4 × wall run (15 seconds each) (see chapter 8). Rest 30 seconds between runs.

3 × crosscourt sprint and shoot (see chapter 8). Shoot 5 free throws between sets.

5 × four corner drill (see chapter 8). Rest 90 seconds between sets.

8 to 10 × viper jumps (tubing; see chapter 7). Rest 10 to 15 seconds between jumps.

Make 100 shots.

PRESEASON PHASE I

WEDNESDAY

Resistance training

EXERCISE	SETS × REPS (% 1RM OR INTENSITY)
Light stretching	10 minutes
Hang clean	3 × 5 (80 to 85%)
Front squat	3 × 5 (70, 75, 80%)
Push press	3 × 5 (70, 75, 80%)
Dumbbell push-up, press, and twist	3 to 6 on each side
Lat pull-down (Swiss ball) (CS)	3 × 5 (80 to 85%)
Biceps curl (CS)	3 × 6 (80 to 85%)
Back extension	3 × 15
Heel raise	4 × 10 (80 to 85%)

Skill and agility training

Ball-handling drills for 10 minutes

Light stretching for 5 minutes

4 × home base drill (20 seconds each). Rest 40 seconds between sets.

3 × wall quick feet (15 seconds each). Rest 15 seconds between sets.

4 × lane agility box drill. Rest 30 seconds between sets.

Make 100 shots.

THURSDAY

Conditioning and skill training

Running warm-ups

Light stretching for 5 minutes

Ball-handling drills for 10 minutes

Rebounder cross the lane, shoot, and sprint

3 to 4 × shooting W drill (see chapter 8). Rest 30 seconds between sets.

2 × 17 drill (see chapter 8). Rest 3 minutes between runs.

12 to 16 × medicine ball wall throw. Rest 15 seconds between throws.

Harness run (tubing; see chapter 7)

Make 100 to 125 shots.

FRIDAY

Resistance training

EXERCISE	SETS × REPS (% 1RM OR INTENSITY)
Abdominal work	4 × 15 to 30
Light stretching	5 minutes
Dumbbell bench press (SS)	3 × 5 (80 to 85%)
Medicine ball chest pass (SS)	3 × 5 (10- to 20-lb medicine ball)
Leg extension	2 × 10 (75 to 80%)
Box squat (PW)	4 × 5 (65, 75, 85, 85%)
(SW)	4 × 5 (65, 70, 75, 75%)
Bench step-up (SS)	3 × 6 (10- to 25-lb dumbbells)
Machine leg curl (SS)	3 × 6 (80 to 85%)
Dumbbell split jump	4 × 8 jumps (10- to 25-lb dumbbells)
Dumbbell hammer curl	3 × 6 (80 to 85%)
Reverse triceps push-up (PW)	3 × 6 (weighted)
(SW)	3 × to failure (no weight)

Skill and agility training

Ball-handling drills for 10 minutes

Light stretching for 5 minutes

4 × home base drill (20 seconds each). Rest 40 seconds between sets.

3 × lateral box jump (25 seconds each). Rest 50 seconds between sets.

2 × half-court layup agility drill (see chapter 9). Shoot 10 free throws between sets.

Make 100 shots.

SATURDAY

Conditioning and skill training

Running warm-ups

Light stretching for 5 minutes

8 × uphill sprint. Walk back down the hill for rest.

Ball-handling drills for 10 minutes

Make 100 shots (optional).

15-point free throw game

Full-court pickup game

Week 25   **Preseason**

MONDAY

Resistance training	
EXERCISE	**SETS × REPS (% 1RM OR INTENSITY)**
Abdominal work	3 × circuit of 3 exercises of 15 to 30 reps (rest 30 seconds between sets)
Light stretching	5 minutes
Bench press (CS) (PW)	4 × 5 (65, 75, 85, 85%)
(SW)	4 × 5 (65, 70, 75, 75%)
Single-arm pullover (CS)	3 × 6
Dumbbell fly	3 × 5 to 6 (80 to 85%)
Leg extension	2 × 10 (75 to 80%)
Squats or leg press (PW)	4 × 5 to 6 (65, 75, 85, 85%)
(SW)	4 × 5 (65, 70, 75, 75%)
Body blade (SS)	15 seconds each leg
Crossover side step-up (SS)	3 × 6 each side (10- to 25-lb dumbbells)
Romanian deadlift	3 × 6 (80 to 85%)
Triceps cable push-down	3 × 6 to 8 (75 to 80%)
Ball-handling drill	Choose 1 from pages 201 to 204.

Agility and footwork

3 × wall quick feet (15 seconds each). Rest 15 seconds between sets.

4 × lane agility box drill. Rest 20 seconds between sets.

3 × reverse 7 drill (see chapter 9). Rest 30 seconds between sets.

3 × cone or minihurdle jump (10 to 15 seconds each). Rest 10 to 15 seconds between sets.

Make 100 shots.

15-point free throw game

TUESDAY

Conditioning and skill training

Running warm-ups

Light stretching for 5 minutes

Ball-handling drills for 10 minutes

2 to 3 × sidewinder drill. Rest 30 seconds between sets.

3 × backboard slap and sprint (see chapter 8). Shoot 5 free throws between sets.

3 × 55-second drill (see chapter 8). Rest 2 minutes between sets.

2 × 300-yard shuttle (see chapter 8). Rest 3 minutes between sets.

10 to 12 × medicine ball squat throw. Rest 30 seconds between throws.

Make 100 shots.

WEDNESDAY

Resistance training

EXERCISE	SETS × REPS (% 1RM OR INTENSITY)
Light stretching	10 minutes
Hang clean	3 × 5 (80 to 85%)
Front squat	3 × 5 (70, 75, 80%)
Push press	3 × 5 (70, 75, 80%)
Dumbbell push-up press and twist (SS)	3 × 3 to 6 on each side
Machine or cable row (SS) (PW)	3 × 5 to 6 (85 to 90%)
(SW)	3 × 5 to 6 (80 to 85%)
Dumbbell hammer curl	3 × 6 (80 to 85%)
Good morning	3 × 10 (75 to 80%)
Heel raise	4 × 10 (80 to 85%)
Ball-handling drill	Choose 1 from pages 201 to 204.
Light stretching	5 minutes

Agility and footwork

3 × wall quick feet (15 seconds each leg). Rest 15 seconds between sets.

3 × lane slide (25 seconds each). Rest 1 minute between runs.

8 to 10 × tennis ball drop (see chapter 9)

5 to 6 × pattern run (I or II). Rest 1 minute between sets.

Make 100 shots.

Shoot 30 to 50 free throws (keep a record of how many you make).

THURSDAY

Conditioning and skill training

Running warm-ups

Light stretching for 5 minutes

Ball-handling drills for 10 minutes

3 × 4, 8, 16 drill. Rest 3 minutes between sets.

4 × circle pass (see chapter 8). Rest 15 seconds between sets.

2 × backboard slap and sprint. Rest 30 to 45 seconds between sets.

25 to 30 × opposite hand layup (see chapter 8) or continue for 4 to 5 minutes.

8 to 10 × viper jump. Rest 10 to 15 seconds between jumps.

10 to 12 × medicine ball squat throw. Rest 30 seconds between throws.

Make 100 shots.

15-point free throw game

PRESEASON PHASE I

FRIDAY

Resistance training

EXERCISE	SETS × REPS (% 1RM OR INTENSITY)
Abdominal work	4 × 15 to 30
Light stretching	5 minutes
Dumbbell incline press (SS) (PW)	3 × 5 (85 to 90%)
(SW)	3 × 5 (80 to 85%)
Basketball push-up (SS)	3 × to failure
Leg extension	2 × 10 (75 to 80%)
Box squat (PW)	4 × 5 to 6 (65, 75, 85, 85%)
(SW)	4 × 5 to 6 (65, 70, 75, 75%)
Dumbbell split jump	4 × 8 jumps (10- to 25-lb dumbbells)
Power slide (bar or band)	2 × 3 to 4 slides each side
Romanian deadlift	3 × 6 (80 to 85%)
Dumbbell triceps extension	3 × 6 to 8 (80 to 85%)
Dumbbell hammer curl	3 × 6 to 8 (80 to 85%)
Ball-handling drill	Choose 1.
Light stretching	5 minutes

Agility and footwork

3 × home base drill (20 seconds each). Rest 40 seconds between sets.

3 × triangle slide. Rest 40 seconds between sets.

3 × star agility drill. Rest 40 seconds between sets.

5 to 6 × pattern run (I or II). Rest 1 minute between sets.

Make 100 shots.

Shoot 30 to 50 free throws (keep a record of how many you make).

SATURDAY

Conditioning and skill training

Running warm-ups

Light stretching for 5 minutes

10 × uphill sprint. Walk back down the hill for rest.

Ball-handling drills for 10 minutes

Make 100 shots (optional).

15-point free throw game

Full-court pickup game

Week 26 **Preseason**

MONDAY

Resistance training

EXERCISE	SETS × REPS (% 1RM OR INTENSITY)
Abdominal work	4 × 15 to 30
Light stretching	5 minutes
Bench press (SS) (PW)	4 × 3 (65, 75, 90. 90%)
(SW)	4 × 4 (65, 70, 75, 75%)
Dip (SS) (PW)	3 × 3 (weighted)
(SW)	3 × to failure
Medicine ball chest pass	3 × 5 throws (10- to 25-lb medicine ball)
Leg extension	2 × 10 (80 to 85%)
Squat or leg press (PW)	3 × 3 to 4 (65, 75, 85, 90%)
(SW)	3 × 3 to 4 (65, 70, 75, 75%)
Box jump-up	3 × 4 jumps (24- to 32-in. box height)
Machine leg curl	3 × 4 (85 to 90%)
Reverse triceps push-up (PW)	3 × 5 to 8 (weight in lap for more resistance)
(SW)	3 × to failure
Ball-handling drill	Choose 1.
Light stretching	5 minutes

Agility and footwork

Jump rope routine

3 × home base drill (20 seconds each). Rest 30 seconds between sets.

3 × reverse 7 drill. Rest 30 seconds between sets.

3 × half-court layup agility drill. Rest by shooting 5 free throws between sets.

Make 100 shots.

TUESDAY

Conditioning and skill training

Running warm-ups

Light stretching for 5 minutes

Ball-handling drills for 10 minutes

Harness run, 12 to 16 × medicine ball wall throw, 2 × 17 drill. Rest 3 minutes between sets.

Make 100 shots.

15-point free throw game

Resistance training

EXERCISE	SETS × REPS (% 1RM OR INTENSITY)
Light stretching	10 minutes
Hang clean (PW)	3 × 3 (85 to 90%)
(SW)	3 × 3 (80 to 85%)
Front squat (PW)	3 × 3 (85 to 90%)
(SW)	3 × 3 (80 to 85%)
Push press (PW)	3 × 3 (85 to 90%)
(SW)	3 × 3 (80 to 85%)
Swiss ball lat pull-down (SS)	3 × 3 to 6 (75 to 80%)
Dumbbell front shoulder raise (SS)	3 × 3 to 6 (75 to 80%)
Reverse arm curl (with bar)	3 × 3 to 6 (75 to 80%)
Reverse hyperextension	3 × 15 to 20
Ball-handling drill	Choose 1.
Light stretching	5 minutes

WEDNESDAY

Agility and footwork

Jump rope routine

3 × home base drill (30 seconds each). Rest 40 seconds between sets.

8 to 10 × tennis ball drop

3 × lateral box jump (25 seconds each). Rest 1 minute between sets.

Make 100 shots.

Shoot 30 to 50 free throws (keep a record of how many you make).

Conditioning and skill training

Running warm-ups

Light stretching for 5 minutes

Ball-handling drills for 10 minutes

4 × wall runs (15 seconds each). Rest 30 seconds between sets.

5 × gassers (see chapter 8). Rest 90 seconds between runs.

3 to 4 × shooting W. Rest 30 seconds between sets.

25 to 30 × opposite hand layup. Shoot 10 layups between sets.

2 to 3 × sidewinder drill. Rest 30 seconds between sets.

3 to 4 × 8 to 10 medicine ball squat press. Rest 10 to 15 seconds between sets.

Make 100 shots.

15-point free throw game

THURSDAY

Week 26   *(continued)*

FRIDAY

Resistance training	
EXERCISE	**SETS × REPS (% 1RM OR INTENSITY)**
Abdominal work	3 × circuit of 3 exercises of 15 to 30 reps (rest 30 seconds between sets)
Light stretching	5 minutes
Dumbbell bench press (PW)	3 × 3 to 4 (85 to 90%)
(SW)	3 × 3 to 4 (80 to 85%)
Medicine ball pullover and throw (SS)	3 × 4 (10- to 25-lb medicine ball)
Dumbbell fly (SS)	3 × 4 to 5 (80 to 85%)
Leg extension	2 × 10 (75 to 80%)
Walking lunge (bar or medicine ball)	3 × 25 yards (75 to 80%)
Bench step-up (single-leg)	3 × 10 (10- to 25-lb dumbbells)
Dumbbell leg curl (SS)	3 × 6 (80 to 85%)
Dumbbell split jump (SS)	4 × 8 jumps (10- to 25-lb dumbbells)
Dumbbell hammer curl (single-leg on Airex pad)	3 × 6 each leg (80 to 85%)
Triceps cable push-down	3 × 10 (75 to 80%)
Ball-handling drill	Choose 1.
Light stretching	5 minutes

Agility and footwork

3 × home base drill (20 seconds each). Rest 40 seconds between sets.

3 × wall quick feet (15 seconds each). Rest 15 seconds between sets.

4 × lane agility box drill. Rest 20 seconds between sets.

5 to 6 × pattern run (I or II). Rest 1 minute between sets.

Make 100 shots.

Shoot 30 to 50 free throws (keep a record of how many you make).

SATURDAY

Conditioning and skill training

Running warm-ups

Light stretching for 5 minutes

10 × uphill sprint. Walk back down the hill for rest.

Ball-handling drills

Make 100 shots.

15-point free throw game

Full-court pickup game

MONDAY

Resistance training

EXERCISE	SETS × REPS (% 1RM OR INTENSITY)
Abdominal work	3 × circuit of 3 exercises of 15 to 30 reps (rest 30 seconds between sets)
Light stretching	5 minutes
Floor bench press (CS) (PW)	4 × 3 (65, 75, 90, 90%)
(SW)	4 × 4 (65, 70, 75, 75%)
Single-arm pullover (CS)	4 × 6
Dumbbell incline press (PW)	3 × 3 (85 to 90%)
(SW)	3 × 3 (80 to 85%)
Leg extension	2 × 10 (75 to 80%)
Leg press (single-leg) (SS) (PW)	3 × 8 (4 right, 4 left) (80 to 85%)
(SW)	3 × 8 (4 right, 4 left) (75 to 80%)
Power slide (bar and band) (SS)	3 × 3 to 4 slides each side
Romanian deadlift	3 × 4 to 5 (80 to 85%)
Dumbbell hammer curl (SS)	3 × 6 (80 to 85%)
Triceps cable push-down (SS)	3 × 10 to 12 (75 to 80%)
Ball-handling drill	Choose 1.
Light stretching	5 minutes

Agility and footwork

3 × dot drill. Rest 45 to 60 seconds between sets.

3 × lateral box jump. Rest 25 seconds between sets.

3 × star agility drill. Rest 30 seconds between sets.

3 × cone or minihurdle jump (10 to 15 seconds each). Rest 10 to 15 seconds between sets.

Make 100 shots.

Shoot 30 to 50 free throws (keep a record of how many you make).

TUESDAY

Conditioning and skill training

Running warm-ups

Light stretching for 5 minutes

Ball-handling drills for 10 minutes

4 × wall runs (15 seconds each). Rest 2 minutes between sets.

2 × 300-yard shuttle. Rest 3 minutes between shuttles.

2 × 55-second drill

8 to 10 × viper jump. Rest 10 to 15 seconds between jumps.

12 to 16 × medicine ball wall throw. Rest 15 seconds between throws.

Make 100 shots.

15-point free throw game

WEDNESDAY

Resistance training

EXERCISE	SETS × REPS (% 1RM OR INTENSITY)
Light stretching	10 minutes
Hang clean (PW)	3 × 3 (85 to 90%)
(SW)	3 × 3 (80 to 85%)
Front squat (PW)	3 × 3 (85 to 90%)
(SW)	3 × 3 (80 to 85%)
Push press (PW)	3 × 3 (85 to 90%)
(SW)	3 × 3 (80 to 85%)
Lat pull-down (PW)	3 × 4 to 6 (85 to 90%)
(SW)	3 × 4 to 6 (80 to 85%)
Dumbbell side raise (single-leg)	3 × 8 (80 to 85%)
Biceps curl	3 × 4 to 6 (80 to 85%)
Back extension	3 × 15
Heel raise	4 × 10 (80 to 85%)
Ball-handling drill	Choose 1.
Light stretching	5 minutes

Agility and footwork

3 × dot drill. Rest 30 to 45 seconds between sets.

3 × lateral box jump. Rest 25 seconds between sets.

3 × quick feet box step. Rest 30 second between sets.

3 × lane slide (25 seconds each). Rest 1 minute between sets.

Make 100 shots.

Shoot 30 to 50 free throws (keep a record of how many you make).

THURSDAY

Conditioning and skill training

Running warm-ups

Light stretching for 5 minutes

Ball-handling drills for 10 minutes

4 × wall runs (15 seconds each). Rest 30 seconds between sets.

2 × 17 drill. Rest 3 minutes between sets.

25 to 30 × opposite hand layup. Shoot 10 free throws between sets.

Harness run

3 to 4 × 8 to 10 medicine ball squat press. Rest 10 to 15 seconds between sets.

Make 100 shots.

15-point free throw game

Week 27   *(continued)*

FRIDAY

Resistance training

EXERCISE	SETS × REPS (% 1RM OR INTENSITY)
Abdominal work	4 × 15 to 30
Light stretching	5 minutes
Single-arm pullover	3 × 6 to 8
Dip (PW)	3 × 3 to 6 (weighted)
(SW)	3 × to failure (no weight)
Medicine ball chest pass (SS)	3 × 6
Leg extension (W)	2 × 10 (75 to 80%)
Single-leg squat	3 × 4 to 5 (75 to 80%)
Box jump-up (SS)	3 × 4 to 5 (24- to 32-in. box height)
Machine leg curl (SS)	3 × 5 to 6 (80 to 85%)
Reverse arm curl (with bar) (SS)	3 × 5 to 6 (80 to 85%)
Dumbbell kickback (SS)	3 × 5 to 8 (75 to 80%)

Agility and footwork

Ball-handling drills for 10 minutes

Light stretching for 5 minutes

3 × dot drill. Rest 45 to 60 seconds between sets.

3 × home base drill (20 seconds each). Rest 40 seconds between sets.

5 to 6 × pattern run (I or II). Rest 1 minute between sets.

2 × half-court layup agility drill. Shoot 10 free throws.

Make 100 shots.

Shoot 30 to 50 free throws (keep a record of how many you make).

SATURDAY

Conditioning and skill training

Running warm-ups

Light stretching for 5 minutes

10 × uphill sprint. Walk back down the hill for rest.

Ball-handling drills for 10 minutes

Make 100 shots.

15-point free throw game

Full-court pickup game

Preseason Phase II—Training Camp

Now we enter the first two weeks of scheduled practice. These two weeks are phase II of the preseason and are also called training camp. Sometime during the first week of practice, test yourself once again to see the improvements you have made during the preseason training up until now. Testing at this point does not need to be as extensive as in the off-season because you will want to be fresh for training camp. I suggest testing body weight, body fat percentage, sit and reach (flexibility), and vertical jump.

To find your improvement on the bench press and squat or leg press, simply take the weight lifted during the last workout that you did on those lifts (90%) and use the repetition maximum formula from chapter 1, pages 7 to 9.

Coaches have many decisions to make leading up to the first week of practice. Being organized is the first ingredient to any successful practice session. During my career I have worked with many successful high school, college, and professional-level basketball coaches who taught me what makes a successful preseason training camp. The training camp is a time of total commitment by athletes and coaching staff. I have always thought it best to take off from resistance work during the first week of practice to concentrate solely on the skills of the game and the conditioning that players need during this time.

Coaches may want to select a conditioning test to see the basketball fitness levels of each athlete. Many different conditioning tests are available to evaluate players' conditioning status. However, I have found that the 300-yard shuttle is a great baseline conditioning test for basketball (see chapter 1). Do this test a day or two before your first day of practice or on the first day of practice in-season, whichever fits your schedule and time frame.

Table 3.2 shows an overview of the first week of training camp. I have also included conditioning testing sessions on Wednesday and Friday (see chapter 8 for details). You can do these sessions before or after practice.

Table 3.2 First Week of Training Camp

Monday	Tuesday	Wednesday	Thursday	Friday	Saturday
Running warm-ups	Running warm-ups	Running warm-ups	Running warm-ups	Running warm-ups	Running warm-ups
Stretch 10 minutes	Stretch 10 minutes	Stretch 10 tminutes	Stretch 10 minutes	Stretch 10 minutes	Stretch 10 minutes
300-yard shuttle test	Practice	17 drill conditioning test	Practice	Gassers conditioning test	Practice
Stretch 10 minutes	Cool down, stretch	Stretch 10 minutes	Cool down, stretch	Stretch 10 minutes	Cool down, stretch
Practice		Practice		Practice	
Cool down, stretch		Cool down, stretch		Cool down, stretch	

Ball-handling drills can be performed before or during practice.

Resistance Training

Your resistance training work resumes during the second week of phase II with two circuit training sessions working the major muscle groups only (see chapter 7). This workout is short but intense and is a good way to get back into the resistance training mode and prepare you for your in-season workouts.

Your training loads during this last preseason week are light (70 to 75%) to moderately light (75 to 80%) for both power work (PW) and speed work (SW). Continue to concentrate on speed of movement, but remember to control the weight; don't jerk or bounce the weight. Use good form on both the concentric (pushing or pulling of the weight) and eccentric portions of the movement (letting the weight back down easily and under control). Your workout should last no more that 30 minutes during this phase to help keep your energy stores and recovery up. Keeping your energy stores up will help your performance on the court.

The schedule also calls for a maximum amount of stretching. I find that most college players who come to the NBA or WNBA are stunned to find out how much stretching players do at this level. To a strength and conditioning coach this is the most important part of a player's program at this time. Take time to stretch! You will see and feel the benefits. Chapter 6 provides flexibility details on each stretch.

Conditioning and Skill Training

During the second week of training camp, conditioning and skill work are still top priorities. Your conditioning, however, is scaled back to only twice a week at this point to give your legs a chance to feel refreshed before your first game (which is coming up shortly).

You only do two days a week of change-of-direction and footwork drills during the second week of training camp. You further taper off to just once a week during the first part of your in-season workouts (see chapter 4).

Plyometric, or jump training, drills are not included in your workouts during these last two weeks of the preseason or during the in-season because of the stress these drills place on the knees. The only jumping drills you will perform during the upcoming phase are those found in your agility and footwork movements, such as dot drills, lateral box jumps, and the cone or minihurdle jumps. Limit these drills to once a week or every two weeks.

Never stop practicing your work toward making the basketball become a part of you and making it do what you want it to do. Even at the professional level, players are always working on this part of their game. You can do this in a short time (5 to 10 minutes) before or after practice with ball-handling drills.

Week 28 Preseason

Rest week from resistance training and conditioning. See practice schedule of first week on page 77.

Week 29 Preseason

MONDAY

Conditioning*

Running warm-ups (see chapter 1)

Stretching for 10 minutes

2 × 300-yard shuttle. Rest 5 minutes between shuttles. Record times and take the average.

1 × 17 drill or gassers (select one). Rest 2:30 to 2:45 between sets.

Cool down and stretch for 10 minutes before the start of practice.

* May be done after practice instead of before.

TUESDAY

Resistance training

Total body circuit × 3. Rest 60 to 90 seconds between groups.

FIRST GROUP OF EXERCISES	SETS × REPS (% 1RM OR INTENSITY)
Bench press	3 × 10 (65, 70, 70%)
Go directly to squat or leg press.	3 × 10 (65, 70, 70%)
Go directly to lateral box jump.	3 × 20 seconds
Go directly to lat pull-down.	3 × 10 (75 to 80%)

Rest 60 to 90 seconds; then repeat circuit twice more.

SECOND GROUP OF EXERCISES	SETS × REPS (% 1RM OR INTENSITY)
Push press	3 × 8 (65, 70, 75%)
Go directly to machine leg curl.	3 × 10 (75 to 80%)
Go directly to Swiss ball walkout push-up.	3 × to failure
Go directly to power shrug or hang clean.	3 × 8 (75 to 80%)

Rest 60 to 90 seconds; then repeat circuit twice more.

WEDNESDAY

Conditioning

Running warm-ups

Stretching for 10 minutes

300-yard shuttle

17 drill or gassers (select one)

Cool down and stretch for 10 minutes before the start of practice.

PRESEASON PHASE II

THURSDAY

Resistance training

Total body circuit × 3. Rest 60 to 90 seconds between groups.

FIRST GROUP OF EXERCISES	SETS × REPS (% 1RM OR INTENSITY)
Dumbbell incline press or machine incline	3 × 10 (75 to 80%)
Go directly to leg press or box squat.	3 × 10 (65, 75, 75%)
Go directly to dot drill.	3 × 30 seconds or less
Go directly to Swiss ball chin-up.	3 × to failure

Rest 60 to 90 seconds; then repeat circuit twice more.

SECOND GROUP OF EXERCISES	SETS × REPS (% 1RM OR INTENSITY)
Dumbbell side raise (single-leg)	3 × 8 (4 right, 4 left) (70 to 75%)
Go directly to straight-leg deadlift.	3 × 8 (75 to 80%)
Go directly to dumbbell hammer curl.	3 × 8 (4 right, 4 left) (75 to 80%)
Go directly to triceps cable push-down.	3 × 10 to 12 (70 to 75%)

Rest 60 to 90 seconds; then repeat circuit twice more.

Sharpening Your Game: In-Season Workouts

After the first two weeks of training camp you officially go into your in-season workouts. This is not a time to simply maintain what you have worked so hard for during the off- and preseason workouts; this is a time to get better and work out to *win!*

Your in-season program lasts 19 weeks, the last week of which is an off week before the start of your conference tournaments. The 19 weeks are broken into two phases:

Phase I, weeks 30 to 42 (13 weeks)

Phase II, weeks 43 to 48 (6 weeks)

Throughout both phases your workouts consist of two weight training sessions and two conditioning sessions each week. The conditioning sessions may include regular conditioning drills, agility and footwork drills, or even some tubing or resistance running and jumping exercises. Either way you have various drills to choose from depending on your needs at the time.

I have designed the in-season workout weeks a little differently from those of the previous phases in that the workouts are not listed by day of the week, but rather as resistance training days 1 and 3 and conditioning and agility training days 2 and 4. Using this format you can determine which workouts are best for your schedule. For example, since most high schools play on Tuesdays and Fridays, you can select your weight training days to be on Mondays and Wednesdays. If you want to avoid doing your resistance work the day before the game, you can choose to resistance train on Wednesdays and Saturdays. College players, on the other hand, may have an entirely different situation in which games are played on any given day as in the NBA and WNBA. In this case you can choose when to do your resistance and conditioning sessions and can adjust the schedule from week to week.

In-Season Phase I

You always play the game the way you practice the game, and you always play with the same intensity as you work out. Whether you are doing ball-handling skills, agility work, or weight training sessions, do not just go through the motions—work out and train throughout this phase to improve your skills and strengths.

Resistance Training

In-season resistance training continues to follow a periodization model as did the off-season and preseason training (see chapter 7 for details on exercises). Training loads typically range from 75 to 85% for both the power work (PW) and the speed work (SW) during this phase. This moderate intensity helps keep the joints fresh and feeling good throughout the long season. Workouts during resistance training sessions are short but intense, much like those of the training camp sessions. During this phase you concentrate on your major muscle groups since they require more energy and are so important in the forceful movement of the game of basketball. The in-season resistance training program includes a variety of workouts; however, all workouts are total body since you are only training twice a week.

Remember that if you perform the sets and complete the reps with the weight percentage required on your core lifts (bench press, push press, squat, or leg press) at any time during your in-season workouts, you now have a new maximum on that particular exercise. You can go up 5 pounds on your bench press or push press, 10 pounds on your squat, and 10 to 20 pounds on your leg press.

There is no resistance training during the 10th week (week 39) of this phase.

Conditioning

In-season conditioning is somewhat different from the conditioning covered in previous chapters. During the in-season phase, conditioning consists of short but intense sport-specific and agility or foot-quickness drills. I have selected these drills to give you the best chance to be at peak condition when the regular season ends and tournament time begins. The one thing that coaches and athletes alike want to avoid is burnout during the middle or the end of the season caused by working too hard. The way to outperform your opponents is not necessarily by working harder, but by working smarter than they do. This smart work ensures that you and your team stay in top condition while remaining fresh and ready to play at your very best throughout the season.

Your in-season conditioning work (see chapter 8 for drills) along with agility and foot-quickness drills (chapter 9) are scheduled for two days each week. Working on agility and foot-quickness during the season helps you stay sharp, focused, and ready to out-hustle your opponent. On some days your coach may want to do one or the other (conditioning or agility) depending on time considerations and how the team is feeling and responding. I like doing agility and conditioning

Ball-handling skills are critical at all levels of play.

work at the end of a practice session because it makes players move quickly when they are tired, something they have to do in the game.

The agility work I suggest for the in-season is a combination of change-of-direction work that is basketball specific. Whichever agility or quickness drill you select, make sure you perform it with an all-out effort. Remember, if you want to be fast, you must train fast, even during the in-season! There is no conditioning training during the 10th and 12th weeks (weeks 39 and 41) of this phase.

Skill Training

Throughout the in-season, you will want to continue working on ball-handling drills. Even the pros work on ball handling throughout the in-season. It's always good to sharpen your skills no matter what position you're playing. If you want to excel at the game, work at the things you are not as good at. Don't be afraid to mess up; that is how you get better.

Most basketball programs include ball-handling as part of regular in-season practice. For this reason, I have not included specific ball-handling drills in the in-season workout tables. If your program doesn't include ball handling during practice, however, I recommend that you work in such drills on your own before or after practice three days a week. Keeping drills fun and competitive during the season is a good way to sharpen skills without pressure. This keeps you loose and can also bring players together. Drills that add variety to the practice schedule are always a plus. You're having fun, but in the meantime you're also getting better while playing different games that are a small but important part of the big picture.

FREE THROW GOLF

This is a great game to play in-season, after your practice session, with two to four players. Each player gets two free throws (from the free throw line), which equal one hole played; you may play 9 or 18 holes. The player with the lowest score wins.

- A shot hitting "nothing but net" equals a birdie or one under par.
- A shot going in but hitting the rim equals par.
- A missed shot equals a bogey or one over par.

Example—Player A hits nothing but net on the first shot and so is one under par. On player A's second shot the ball goes in but hits the rim for par; player A is still one under par. Player B steps up and both shots are nothing but net. Player B is now two under par, and the first hole is complete.

DAY 1

Resistance training

EXERCISE	SETS × REPS (% 1RM OR INTENSITY)
Core work	Choose one exercise from chapter 7 (pages 135 to 138).
Light stretching	5 minutes
Circuit training—group 1*	
Dumbbell bench press	1 × 10 (75 to 80%)
Go directly to leg press.	1 × 12 (75 to 80%)
Go directly to lat pull-down.	1 × 10 (75 to 80%)
Go directly to push press.	1 × 8 (75 to 80%)
*After completing group 1 twice, go to group 2.	
Circuit training—group 2	
Basketball push-up	1 × to failure
Go directly to machine leg curl.	1 × 10 (70 to 75%)
Go directly to dumbbell hammer curl.	1 × 10 (70 to 75%)

DAY 2

Conditioning and agility training

Before, during, or after practice:

5 × lane slides (see chapter 9). Rest 30 seconds between sets

After practice:

5 × 30-second gassers (see chapter 8). Rest 90 seconds between sets.

DAY 3

Resistance training

EXERCISE	SETS × REPS (% 1RM OR INTENSITY)
Core work	Choose 1 exercise from chapter 7.
Light stretching	10 minutes
Dumbbell incline press (SS)	3 × 10 (80 to 85%)
Swiss ball balance push-up (SS)	3 × to failure
Hang clean to front squat to push press	3 × 8 (75 to 80%)
Lat pull-down	3 × 8 to 10 (75 to 80%)
Straight-leg deadlift	3 × 8 (70 to 75%)
Heel raise	3 × 8 to10 (75 to 80%)

DAY 4

Conditioning and agility training

Before, during, or after practice:

3 × dot drill (see chapter 9). Rest 60 seconds between sets.

After practice:

4 to 5 × four corner drill (see chapter 8). Rest 90 seconds between sets.

Week 31   **In-Season**

<table>
<tr><td rowspan="7">DAY 1</td><td colspan="2">Resistance training</td></tr>
<tr><td>EXERCISE</td><td>SETS × REPS (% 1RM OR INTENSITY)</td></tr>
<tr><td>Abdominal work</td><td>2 × circuit of 3 exercises from pages 131 to 135.</td></tr>
<tr><td>Metabolic work</td><td>3 × 3 with 60 to 90 seconds between each tri-set</td></tr>
<tr><td>Squat or leg press</td><td>15, 12, 10 (reps)</td></tr>
<tr><td>Bench press or dumbbell incline press</td><td>12, 10, 8 (reps)</td></tr>
<tr><td>Machine row or lat pull-down</td><td>12, 10, 8 (reps)</td></tr>
<tr><td>Reverse hyperextension</td><td>3 × 15</td></tr>
</table>

<table>
<tr><td rowspan="4">DAY 2</td><td colspan="2">Conditioning and agility training</td></tr>
<tr><td colspan="2">Before, during or after practice:

Jump rope routine</td></tr>
<tr><td colspan="2">After practice:</td></tr>
<tr><td colspan="2">3 × ladder sprint (see chapter 8). Rest 90 seconds between sprints.</td></tr>
</table>

<table>
<tr><td rowspan="11">DAY 3</td><td colspan="2">Resistance training</td></tr>
<tr><td>EXERCISE</td><td>SETS × REPS (% 1RM OR INTENSITY)</td></tr>
<tr><td>Core work</td><td>Choose 1 exercise from chapter 7.</td></tr>
<tr><td>Light stretching</td><td>5 minutes</td></tr>
<tr><td>Dumbbell bench press (Swiss ball)</td><td>3 × 10 (75 to 80%)</td></tr>
<tr><td>Leg extension</td><td>2 × 10 (75 to 80%)</td></tr>
<tr><td>Single-leg squat</td><td>3 × 8 (75 to 80%)</td></tr>
<tr><td>Dumbbell leg curl (SS)</td><td>3 × 8 (75 to 80%)</td></tr>
<tr><td>Crossover side step-up (SS)</td><td>3 × 8 (10- to 25-lb dumbbells)</td></tr>
<tr><td>Swiss ball chin-up</td><td>3 × to failure</td></tr>
<tr><td>Heel raise</td><td>3 × 10 (75 to 80%)</td></tr>
</table>

<table>
<tr><td rowspan="4">DAY 4</td><td colspan="2">Conditioning and agility training</td></tr>
<tr><td colspan="2">Before, during, or after practice:</td></tr>
<tr><td colspan="2">2 × home base drill (see chapter 9). Rest 30 to 90 seconds between drills.</td></tr>
<tr><td colspan="2">After practice:

2 × gassers or team free throw and sprint (see chapter 8). Rest 90 seconds between sets.</td></tr>
</table>

IN-SEASON PHASE I

Week 32 In-Season

Resistance training	
EXERCISE	**SETS × REPS (% 1RM OR INTENSITY)**
Core work	Choose 1 exercise.
Light stretching	5 minutes
Rotator cuff work	Choose 1 exercise × 8 to 10 (pages 142 to 144).
Dumbbell bench press	3 × 8 (65, 70, 75%)
Leg extension	2 × 10 (75 to 80%)
Side squat	3 × 8 each leg (75 to 80%)
Machine leg curl (CS)	3 × 8 (75 to 80%)
Lat pull-down or machine or cable row (CS)	3 × 8 (75 to 80%)
Single-leg dumbbell press	3 × 10 (5 right, 5 left) (75 to 80%)
Reverse arm curl (bar)	3 × 8 (70 to 75%)
Heel raise	4 × 10 (75 to 80%)

DAY 1

Conditioning and agility training

DAY 2

Before, during, or after practice:

3 to 4 × lane agility box drill (see chapter 9). Rest 30 to 45 seconds between sets.

After practice:

1 × 300-yard shuttle (see chapter 8) and team free throw and sprint

Resistance training	
EXERCISE	**SETS × REPS (% 1RM OR INTENSITY)**
Light stretching	5 minutes
Hang clean to front squat to push press	3 × 8 (75 to 80%)
Hip abduction with band	2 × 10 each leg
Dumbbell incline press (CS)	3 × 8 (75 to 80%)
Swiss ball chin-up (CS)	3 × to failure
Dumbbell front shoulder raise	3 × 8 (75 to 80%)
Romanian deadlift	3 × 8 (75 to 80%)
Heel raise	4 × 10 (75 to 80%)

DAY 3

Conditioning and agility training

DAY 4

Before, during, or after practice:

3 × home base drill. Rest 30 seconds between sets.

Before or after practice:

1 × 4, 8, 16 drill (see chapter 8). Go right to opposite hand layup drill (see chapter 8).

Week 33 In-Season

Resistance training	
EXERCISE	**SETS × REPS (% 1RM OR INTENSITY)**
Abdominal work	2 × circuit of 3 exercises
Light stretching	5 minutes
Dumbbell incline press (Swiss ball (SS)	3 × 8 (80 to 85%)
Swiss ball balance push-up (SS)	3 × to failure
Box squat or leg press (SS)	4 × 8 (60, 70, 75, 75%)
Power slide (SS)	4 × 3 to 4 slides each side
Romanian deadlift to dumbbell press	3 × 8 (75 to 80%)
Single-arm pullover (Swiss ball)	3 × 6 (using rope for resistance)
Triceps cable push-down (SS)	3 × 8 to 10 (75 to 80%)
Biceps curl (SS)	3 × 8 to 10 (75 to 80%)

DAY 1 (row label)

Conditioning and agility training

DAY 2

Before or after practice:

3 to 4 × four corner drill. Rest 90 seconds between sets. Team free throw and sprint.

Before, during, or after practice:

10 × wall quick feet (see chapter 9). Rest 5 to 10 seconds between sets.

Resistance training	
EXERCISE	**SETS × REPS (% 1RM OR INTENSITY)**
Core work	Choose 1 exercise 3 × 15 to 30
Light stretching	5 minutes
Leg extension	2 × 10 (70 to 75%)
Matrix I (see chapter 7)	3 rounds, 45-second rest between rounds
Leg press (SS)	4 × 10 (65, 70, 75, 75%)
Straight-leg deadlift (SS)	4 × 8 (75 to 80%)
Dumbbell incline press	3 × 8 (75 to 80%)
Lat pull-down	3 × 8 (75 to 80%)
Dumbbell hammer curl to push press	3 × 8 (75 to 80%)

DAY 3

Conditioning and agility training

DAY 4

Before, during, or after practice:

3 to 4 × reverse 7 drill (see chapter 9). Rest 30 seconds between sets.

After practice:

4 × 30-second gassers. Rest 90 seconds between sets.

IN-SEASON PHASE I

Week 34 In-Season

Resistance training	
EXERCISE	**SETS × REPS (% 1RM OR INTENSITY)**
Abdominal work	2 × circuit
Light stretching	5 minutes
Rotator cuff work	Choose 1 exercise × 8 to 10.
Bench press (PW)	4 × 5 (65, 75, 80, 80%)
(SW)	4 × 5 (65, 70, 75, 75%)
Leg extension	2 × 10 (75 to 80%)
Single-leg squat	3 × 5 to 6 (80 to 85%)
Hang clean	3 × 5 (80 to 85%)
Machine or cable row	3 × 5 to 6 (80 to 85%)
Dumbbell rear shoulder raise	3 × 5 to 6 (75 to 80%)
Heel raise	4 × 10 to 12 (80 to 85%)

DAY 1

Conditioning and agility training

DAY 2

Before practice:

4 × wall run (see chapter 8). Rest 30 seconds between runs.

After finishing all 4 wall run sets, go directly to 3 × pattern run I (see chapter 9).

Resistance training	
EXERCISE	**SETS × REPS (% 1RM OR INTENSITY)**
Light stretching	5 minutes
Hang clean to front squat to push press	3 × 5 (80 to 85%)
Matrix II	3 × 2 rounds, 45 seconds rest between rounds
Dumbbell incline press (Swiss ball)	3 × 5 (80 to 85%)
Lat pull-down	3 × 5 to 6 (80 to 85%)
Reverse hyperextension (Swiss ball)	3 × 10 to 15
Heel raise	4 × 10 to 12 (80 to 85%)

DAY 3

Conditioning and agility training

DAY 4

Before or after practice:

2 × backboard slap and sprint (see chapter 8). Go directly to 2 × 55-second drill (see chapter 8). Rest 30 seconds between sets.

After practice:

3 × lane slide. Rest 30 seconds between sets.

Week 35 In-Season

<table>
<tr><td rowspan="2">DAY 1</td><td colspan="2">Resistance training</td></tr>
<tr><td>EXERCISE</td><td>SETS × REPS (% 1RM OR INTENSITY)</td></tr>
<tr><td></td><td>Core work</td><td>Choose 1 exercise 3 × 15 to 30.</td></tr>
<tr><td></td><td>Light stretching</td><td>5 minutes</td></tr>
<tr><td></td><td>Close-grip bench press</td><td>3 × 5 (80 to 85%)</td></tr>
<tr><td></td><td>Medicine ball chest pass (SS)</td><td>3 × 5 (10- to 25-lb medicine ball)</td></tr>
<tr><td></td><td>Dumbbell leg curl (SS)</td><td>3 × 6 (80 to 85%)</td></tr>
<tr><td></td><td>Leg extension (SS)</td><td>3 × 10 (75 to 80%)</td></tr>
<tr><td></td><td>Leg press (PW)</td><td>4 × 6 (65, 75, 80, 80%)</td></tr>
<tr><td></td><td>(SW)</td><td>4 × 6 (65, 70, 75, 75%)</td></tr>
<tr><td></td><td>Swiss ball chin-up</td><td>3 × to failure</td></tr>
<tr><td></td><td>Triceps cable push-down (SS)</td><td>3 × 6 to 10 (75 to 80%)</td></tr>
<tr><td></td><td>Dumbbell hammer curl (SS)</td><td>3 × 6 to 10 (75 to 80%)</td></tr>
</table>

<table>
<tr><td rowspan="4">DAY 2</td><td colspan="2">Conditioning and agility training</td></tr>
<tr><td colspan="2">Before or after practice:

3 × sidewinder drill (tubing; see chapter 7). Rest for 30 seconds between sets.</td></tr>
<tr><td colspan="2">After practice:

1 × ladder sprint. Go directly to 3 × crosscourt sprint and shoot (see chapter 8). Rest 45 seconds between sets or shoot 5 free throws.</td></tr>
</table>

<table>
<tr><td rowspan="2">DAY 3</td><td colspan="2">Resistance training</td></tr>
<tr><td>EXERCISE</td><td>SETS × REPS (% 1RM OR INTENSITY)</td></tr>
<tr><td></td><td>Abdominal work</td><td>2 × circuit</td></tr>
<tr><td></td><td>Light stretching</td><td>5 minutes</td></tr>
<tr><td></td><td>Leg extension</td><td>2 × 10 (75 to 80%)</td></tr>
<tr><td></td><td>Matrix I</td><td>3 × 2 rounds, 45 seconds rest between rounds</td></tr>
<tr><td></td><td>Swiss ball balance push-up</td><td>3 × to failure</td></tr>
<tr><td></td><td>Side lunge</td><td>2 × 6 each side</td></tr>
<tr><td></td><td>Romanian deadlift to dumbbell press</td><td>3 × 6 (80 to 85%)</td></tr>
<tr><td></td><td>Dumbbell hammer curl to dumbbell push press</td><td>3 × 6 (80 to 85%)</td></tr>
<tr><td></td><td>Heel raise</td><td>4 × 10 (80 to 85%)</td></tr>
</table>

<table>
<tr><td rowspan="2">DAY 4</td><td colspan="2">Conditioning and agility training</td></tr>
<tr><td colspan="2">After practice:

4 × 30-second gassers or 4 × team free throw and sprint. Rest 90 seconds between sets.

2 × lateral box jump (20 seconds each) (see chapter 7)</td></tr>
</table>

Resistance training

	EXERCISE	SETS × REPS (% 1RM OR INTENSITY)
DAY 1	Core work	Choose 1 exercise.
	Light stretching	5 minutes
	Rotator cuff work	Choose 1 exercise × 8 to 10.
	Bench press (PW)	4 × 5 (65, 75, 80, 85%)
	(SW)	4 × 5 (65, 70, 75, 75%)
	Chin-up	3 × to failure
	Leg extension	2 × 10 (75 to 80%)
	Squat or leg press (PW)	4 × 5 (65, 75, 80, 85%)
	(SW)	4 × 5 (65, 70, 75, 75%)
	Hip abduction with band	2 × 10 each leg
	Romanian deadlift to dumbbell press	3 × 5 (80 to 85%)
	Reverse arm curl (bar)	3 × 5 to 6 (75 to 80%)
	Heel raise	4 × 10 (80 to 85%)

Conditioning and agility training

DAY 2

Before, during, or after practice:

3 × lane agility box drill. Rest 30 seconds between sets.

After practice:

1 × 4, 8, 16 drill. Go to 1 × opposite hand layup drill.

Resistance training

	EXERCISE	SETS × REPS (% 1RM OR INTENSITY)
DAY 3	Abdominal work	2 × circuit
	Light stretching	5 minutes
	Hang clean to front squat to push press	3 × 5 (75 to 80%)
	Dumbbell bench press (CS)	3 × 5 (80 to 85%)
	Lat pull-down (CS)	3 × 5 to 6 (80 to 85%)
	Matrix II	3 × 2 rounds, 45 seconds rest between rounds
	Reverse hyperextension (on bench)	2 × 15 to 20

Conditioning and agility training

DAY 4

After practice:

3 × wall run. Rest 30 seconds between runs. Directly after wall runs go to 3 × harness run (see chapter 7).

Week 37   **In-Season**

<table>
<tr><td rowspan="13" style="writing-mode: vertical-rl">DAY 1</td><td colspan="2">Resistance training</td></tr>
<tr><td>EXERCISE</td><td>SETS × REPS (% 1RM OR INTENSITY)</td></tr>
<tr><td>Core work</td><td>Choose 1 exercise.</td></tr>
<tr><td>Light stretching</td><td>5 minutes</td></tr>
<tr><td>Floor bench press (SS) (PW)</td><td>3 × 4 (65, 75, 80%)</td></tr>
<tr><td>(SW)</td><td>3 × 4 (65, 70, 75%)</td></tr>
<tr><td>Medicine ball throw on Swiss ball (SS)</td><td>3 × 5 (10- to 20-lb medicine ball)</td></tr>
<tr><td>Leg extension</td><td>2 × 10 (75 to 80%)</td></tr>
<tr><td>Box squat or leg press (PW)</td><td>4 × 4 (65, 75, 80, 85%)</td></tr>
<tr><td>(SW)</td><td>4 × 4 (65, 75, 75, 75%)</td></tr>
<tr><td>Romanian deadlift to dumbbell press</td><td>3 × 4 (80 to 85%)</td></tr>
<tr><td>Dumbbell biceps curl</td><td>3 × 4 to 6 (80 to 85%)</td></tr>
<tr><td>Heel raise</td><td>4 × 10 (80 to 85%)</td></tr>
</table>

<table>
<tr><td rowspan="2" style="writing-mode: vertical-rl">DAY 2</td><td>Conditioning and agility training</td></tr>
<tr><td>After practice:
Team free throws and sprint or 1 × sprint and walk ladder drill (see chapter 8); 2 × dot drill</td></tr>
</table>

<table>
<tr><td rowspan="11" style="writing-mode: vertical-rl">DAY 3</td><td colspan="2">Resistance training</td></tr>
<tr><td>EXERCISE</td><td>SETS × REPS (% 1RM OR INTENSITY)</td></tr>
<tr><td>Abdominal work</td><td>2 × circuit</td></tr>
<tr><td>Light stretching</td><td>5 minutes</td></tr>
<tr><td>Leg extension</td><td>2 × 10 (75 to 80%)</td></tr>
<tr><td>Matrix I</td><td>3 × 2 rounds, 45 seconds rest between rounds</td></tr>
<tr><td>Single-leg squat</td><td>3 × 4 (80 to 85%)</td></tr>
<tr><td>Dumbbell leg curl</td><td>3 × 5 to 6 (80 to 85%)</td></tr>
<tr><td>Dumbbell incline press (Swiss ball) (CS)</td><td>3 × 4 (80 to 85%)</td></tr>
<tr><td>Swiss ball chin-up (CS)</td><td>3 × to failure</td></tr>
<tr><td>Back extension</td><td>3 × 15</td></tr>
</table>

<table>
<tr><td rowspan="2" style="writing-mode: vertical-rl">DAY 4</td><td>Conditioning and agility training</td></tr>
<tr><td>After practice:
Team free throw and sprint or 1 × gassers and/or half-court layup agility drill (see chapter 9)</td></tr>
</table>

Week 38　In-Season

Resistance training	
EXERCISE	**SETS × REPS (% 1RM OR INTENSITY)**
Core work	Choose 1 exercise.
Light stretch	5 minutes
Rotator cuff work	Choose 1 exercise × 8 to 10.
Bench press (PW)	4 × 3 (65, 75, 85, 85%)
(SW)	4 × 3 (65, 75, 80, 80%)
Dumbbell fly	3 × 5 to 6 (80 to 85%)
Lat pull-down) (PW)	3 × 4 (85 to 90%)
(SW)	3 × 4 (80 to 85%)
Leg extension	2 × 10 (75 to 80%)
Box squat (PW)	4 × 3 (65, 75, 85, 85%)
(SW)	4 × 3 (65, 75, 80, 80%)
Machine leg curl (PW)	3 × 4 (85 to 90%)
(SW)	3 × 4 (80 to 85%)
Dumbbell side raise	3 × 4 to 6 (80 to 85%)
Triceps cable push-down (SS)	3 × 6 to 10 (80 to 85%)
Biceps curl (SS)	3 × 4 to 6 (80 to 85%)

DAY 1

Conditioning and agility training

DAY 2

After practice:

4 × four corners drill or 4 × team free throw and sprint. Rest 90 seconds between sets.

3 × sidewinder (tubing). Rest 30 seconds between sets.

Resistance training	
EXERCISE	**SETS × REPS (% 1RM OR INTENSITY)**
Abdominal work	2 × circuit
Light stretching	5 minutes
Hang clean to front squat to push press	3 × 3 (80 to 85%)
Matrix I	3 × 2 rounds, 45 seconds rest between rounds
Single-arm pullover (Swiss ball)	3 × 6 (using rope)
Dumbbell leg curl	3 × 4 (80 to 85%)
Reverse hyperextension (on bench)	3 × 15

DAY 3

Conditioning and agility training

DAY 4

After practice:

3 × backboard slap and sprint. Rest 90 seconds between sets.

Go directly to 3 × quick feet box step drill (see chapter 9). Rest 20 seconds between sets.

Week 39 **In-Season**

Rest week from resistance training and conditioning. Only regular practice this week.

Resistance training	
EXERCISE	**SETS × REPS (% 1RM OR INTENSITY)**
Core work	Choose 1 exercise.
Light stretching	5 minutes
Circuit training—group 1*	
Dumbbell bench press	1 × 10 (75 to 80%)
Go directly to leg press.	1 × 12 (75 to 80%)
Go directly to lat pull-down.	1 × 10 (75 to 80%)
Go directly to push press.	1 × 8 (75 to 80%)
* Rest 90 seconds and repeat twice; then go to group 2.	
Circuit training—group 2*	
Swiss ball balance push-up	
Go directly to machine leg curl.	1 × to failure
Go directly to dumbbell hammer curl	1 × 10 (75 to 80%)
* Rest 60 seconds and repeat twice.	1 × 8 (80 to 85%)

DAY 1

Conditioning and agility training
After practice:
4 × pattern run. Rest 45 seconds between sets.

DAY 2

Resistance training	
EXERCISE	**SETS × REPS (% 1RM OR INTENSITY)**
Abdominal work	Circuit × 3
Light stretching	5 minutes
Circuit training—group 1*	
Dumbbell incline press	1 × 8 (75 to 80%)
Go directly to box squat.	1 × 10 (75 to 80%)
Go directly to machine or cable row.	1 × 10 (80 to 85%)
Go directly to military press (using bar).	1 × 8 (75 to 80%)
* Rest 90 seconds; repeat twice; then go to group 2.	
Circuit training—group 2*	
Basketball push-up	1 × to failure
Go directly to straight-leg deadlift.	1 × to failure
Go directly to reverse arm curl (bar).	1 × 8 (75 to 80%)
* Repeat twice.	1 × 8 (70 to 75%)

DAY 3

Conditioning and agility training
After practice:
3 × 30-second gassers. Rest 90 seconds between sets. Go directly to 4 × sidewinder drill (tubing). Rest 30 seconds between sets.

DAY 4

Week 41 **In-Season**

DAY 1

Resistance training

EXERCISE	SETS × REPS (% 1RM OR INTENSITY)
Core work	Choose 1 exercise.
Light stretching	5 minutes
Leg extension	2 × 10 (75 to 80%)
Squat or leg press	4 × 8 (65, 70, 75, 75%)
Dumbbell leg curl on Swiss ball	3 × 8 (75 to 80%)
Dip	3 × to failure
Single-arm pullover (Swiss ball) (SS)	3 × 6 (using rope)
Military press	3 × 8 (75 to 80%)
Good morning	3 × 8 (70 to 75%)
Machine biceps curl	3 × 8 to 10 (75 to 80%)
Heel raise	4 × 10 (75 to 80%)

DAY 2

Conditioning and agility training

None

DAY 3

Resistance training

EXERCISE	SETS × REPS (% 1RM OR INTENSITY)
Abdominal work	3 × 15 to 30
Light stretching	5 minutes
Dumbbell bench press (CS)	3 × 8 (70 to 80%)
Swiss ball chin-up (CS)	3 × to failure
Leg extension	2 × 10 (75 to 80%)
Hip abduction with band	2 × 10 each leg
Matrix II	2 × 2 rounds, 45-second rest between rounds
Dumbbell hammer curl to dumbbell push press	3 × 8 (75 to 80%)
Machine leg curl	3 × 8 (75 to 80%)
Back extension	3 × 15
Heel raise	4 × 10 (75 to 80%)

DAY 4

Conditioning and agility training

None

Week 42 **In-Season**

DAY 1

Resistance training	
EXERCISE	**SETS × REPS (% 1RM OR INTENSITY)**
Core work	Choose 1 exercise.
Light stretching	5 minutes
Rotator cuff work	Choose 1 exercise × 8 to 10).
Bench press (PW)	4 × 5 (65, 75, 80, 85%)
(SW)	4 × 5 (65, 70, 75, 75%)
Machine or cable row (PW)	3 × 5 (85 to 90%)
(SW)	3 × 5 (80 to 85%)
Leg extension	3 × 10 (75 to 80%)
Box squat or leg press (PW)	4 × 5 (65, 75, 80, 85%)
(SW)	4 × 5 (65, 70, 75, 75%)
Romanian deadlift to dumbbell press	3 × 5 (80 to 85%)
Heel raise	4 × 10 (80 to 85%)

DAY 2

Conditioning and agility training

Before or after practice:

2 × dot drill; 2 × quick feet box step. Rest 30 seconds between sets.

DAY 3

Resistance training	
EXERCISE	**SETS × REPS (% 1RM OR INTENSITY)**
Abdominal work	Circuit × 2
Light stretching	5 minutes
Dumbbell bench press (SS) (PW)	3 × 5 (85 to 90%)
(SW)	3 × 5 (80 to 85%)
Swiss ball balance push-up (SS)	3 × to failure
Leg extension	2 × 10 (75 to 80%)
Single-leg squat (SS)	3 × 5 (80 to 85%)
Bench step-up (SS)	3 × 5 (10- to 25-lb dumbbells)
Lat pull-down (PW)	3 × 5 (85 to 90%)
(SW)	3 × 5 (80 to 85%)
Machine leg curl	3 × 5 (75 to 80%)
Good morning	3 × 6 to 8 (70 to 75%)

DAY 4

Conditioning and agility training

After practice:

4 × pattern run (I or II). Rest 45 seconds between sets.

In-Season Phase II

The second phase of in-season training is used to prepare specifically for tournament time. Tournament time is when all of your hard work pays off. Hard work may not guarantee success, but without it you don't stand a chance!

Your overall training changes to some degree during this six-week phase. Workouts are shorter because the number of exercises during each workout has been cut back. This "tapering" helps energize your body at just the right time and gives you the added rest you need for the upcoming tournament games.

Resistance Training

Not only has the number of exercises been reduced, but also the number of repetitions of each exercise has been cut back. The scheme of the last phase was from five to eight reps. During phase II of the in-season program exercise reps start at five and go all the way down to three on some exercises. The intensity (weight) used for each exercise stays around 75 to 80% to 85 to 90% on a few exercises.

The exercises during this phase come back somewhat to the basics; that is, they are not as diverse, specialized, or complex as the exercises in previous phases. These basic movements all have an aim of resting the body while maintaining fitness and strength.

Conditioning and Skill Training

As you begin tapering back on workouts in this phase, you also cut back on conditioning and skill training. The first three weeks of this phase (weeks 43 to 45) do not have any conditioning, agility, or skill training. Light conditioning drills reappear in the final three weeks of the phase.

	Resistance training	
	EXERCISE	**SETS × REPS (% 1RM OR INTENSITY)**
DAY 1	Core work	Choose 1 exercise (pages 135 to 138).
	Light stretching	5 minutes
	Hang clean to front squat to push press	3 × 5 (80 to 85%)
	Swiss ball balance push-up (CS)	3 × to failure
	Military press (CS) (PW)	3 × 5 (80 to 85%)
	(SW)	3 × 5 (75 to 80%)
	Chin-up	3 × to failure
	Back extension	3 × 15
	Heel raise	4 × 10 (80 to 85%)

	Conditioning and agility training	
DAY 2	None	

	Resistance training	
	EXERCISE	**SETS × REPS (% 1RM OR INTENSITY)**
DAY 3	Abdominal work	3 × 15 to 30 (pages 131 to 135)
	Light stretching	5 minutes
	Leg extension	2 × 10 (75 to 80%)
	Leg press (PW)	4 × 5 (65, 75, 85, 85%)
	(SW)	4 × 5 (65, 70, 75, 75%)
	Dumbbell bench press (PW)	3 × 5 (85 to 90%)
	(SW)	3 × 5 (80 to 85%)
	Swiss ball chin-up	3 × to failure
	Matrix II	2 × 2 rounds, 45 seconds rest between rounds
	Triceps cable push-down (SS)	3 × 6 to 10 (75 to 80%)
	Biceps curl (SS)	3 × 6 to 10 (75 to 80%)

	Conditioning and agility training	
DAY 4	None	

IN-SEASON PHASE II

Resistance training	
EXERCISE	**SETS × REPS (% 1RM OR INTENSITY)**
Core work	Choose 1 exercise.
Light stretching	5 minutes
Rotator cuff work	Choose 1 exercise × 8 to 10 (see pages 142 to 144).
Bench press (CS) (PW)	4 × 5 (65, 75, 85, 85%)
(SW)	4 × 5 (65, 70, 75, 75%)
Lat pull-down (CS) (PW)	3 × 5 (85 to 90%)
(SW)	3 × 5 (80 to 85%)
Leg extension (SS)	2 × 10 (75 to 80%)
Hip abduction with band (SS)	2 × 10 each leg
Leg press (PW)	4 × 5 (65, 75, 85, 85%)
(SW)	4 × 5 to 6 (65, 70, 75, 75%)
Romanian deadlift to dumbbell press	3 × 5 (80 to 85%)

DAY 1

Conditioning and agility training
None

DAY 2

Resistance training	
EXERCISE	**SETS × REPS (% 1RM OR INTENSITY)**
Abdominal work	2 × circuit
Light stretching	5 minutes
Leg extension	2 × 10 (75 to 80%)
Box squat or leg press (PW)	4 × 5 (65, 75, 85, 85%)
(SW)	4 × 5 (65, 75, 80, 80%)
Military press (CS)	3 × 5 (80 to 85%)
Swiss ball chin-up (CS)	3 × to failure
Triceps cable push-down	3 × 6 to 10 (80 to 85%)
Dumbbell hammer curl	3 × 6 to 10 (80 to 85%)

DAY 3

Conditioning and agility training
None

DAY 4

IN-SEASON PHASE II

Week 45 In-Season

Touch up on your ball-handling skills this week. See the drills in chapter 9, pages 201 to 204.

IN-SEASON PHASE II

DAY 1

Resistance training

EXERCISE	SETS × REPS (% 1RM OR INTENSITY)
Core work	Choose 1 exercise.
Light stretching	5 minutes
Rotator cuff work	Choose 1 exercise × 8 to 10.
Bench press (PW)	4 × 3 (65, 75, 85, 90%)
(SW)	4 × 3 (65, 75, 80, 80%)
Leg extension	2 × 10 (75 to 80%)
Matrix II	2 × 2 rounds, 45 seconds rest between rounds
Lat pull-down (PW)	3 × 4 to 6 (85 to 90%)
(SW)	3 × 4 to 6 (80 to 85%)
Straight-leg deadlift	3 × 6 (80 to 85%)
Reverse hyperextension	3 × 15
Heel raise	4 × 10 (80 to 85%)

DAY 2

Conditioning and agility training

None

DAY 3

Resistance training

EXERCISE	SETS × REPS (% 1RM OR INTENSITY)
Abdominal work	2 × circuit
Light stretching	5 minutes
Leg extension	2 × 10 (75 to 80%)
Leg press (PW)	4 × 4 (65, 75, 85, 90%)
(SW)	4 × 4 (65, 75, 80, 80%)
Dumbbell leg curl	3 × 4 to 6 (85 to 90%)
Dumbbell bench press (PW)	3 × 3 (85 to 90%)
(SW)	3 × 3 (80 to 85%)
Machine or cable row (PW)	3 × 3 to 4 (85 to 90%)
(SW)	3 × 3 to 4 (80 to 85%)
Reverse hyperextension (on bench)	3 × 15

DAY 4

Conditioning and agility training

None

Week 46 **In-Season**

<table>
<tr><td rowspan="11">DAY 1</td><td colspan="2">Resistance training</td></tr>
<tr><td>EXERCISE</td><td>SETS × REPS (% 1RM OR INTENSITY)</td></tr>
<tr><td>Core work</td><td>Choose 1 exercise.</td></tr>
<tr><td>Light stretching</td><td>5 minutes</td></tr>
<tr><td>Floor bench press (PW)</td><td>3 × 3 to 4 (85 to 90%)</td></tr>
<tr><td style="text-align:right">(SW)</td><td>3 × 3 to 4 (80 to 85%)</td></tr>
<tr><td>Swiss ball chin-up (CS)</td><td>3 × to failure</td></tr>
<tr><td>Leg extension (CS)</td><td>2 × 10 (75 to 80%)</td></tr>
<tr><td>Hip abduction with band (SS)</td><td>2 × 10 each leg</td></tr>
<tr><td>Swiss ball leg curl (SS)</td><td>3 × 10 (75 to 80%)</td></tr>
<tr><td>Close-grip bench press (CS)</td><td>3 × 4 (80 to 85%)</td></tr>
</table>

Back extension (on bench) (CS) — 3 × 15
Dumbbell hammer curl — 3 × 6 to 10 (85 to 90%)

DAY 2

Conditioning and agility training

After practice:

2 × dot drill. Rest 30 seconds between each set.

DAY 3

Resistance training

EXERCISE	SETS × REPS (% 1RM OR INTENSITY)
Abdominal work	3 × 15 to 30
Light stretching	5 minutes
Leg extension	2 × 10 (75 to 80%)
Matrix II	2 × 2 rounds, 45 seconds rest between rounds
Machine leg curl	3 × 4 to 6 (80 to 85%)
Dumbbell bench press (PW)	3 × 4 (85 to 90%)
(SW)	3 × 4 (80 to 85%)
Lat pull-down (CS)	3 ×10 (85 to 90%)
Dumbbell hammer curl (single-leg) (CS)	3 × 4 each leg (80 to 85%)
Reverse triceps push-up (CS)	3 × to failure
Back extension (CS)	2 × 15

DAY 4

Conditioning and agility training

After practice:

4 × 1 sidewinder drill (tubing). Rest 30 seconds between sets.

Week 47 In-Season

DAY 1	Resistance training	
	EXERCISE	**SETS × REPS (% 1RM OR INTENSITY)**
	Core work	Choose 1 exercise.
	Light stretching	5 minutes
	Leg extension	2 × 10 (75 to 80%)
	Single-leg squat (SS)	3 × 4 (75 to 80%)
	Hip abduction with band (SS)	3 × 10 each leg
	Dumbbell bench press (PW)	3 × 4 (85 to 90%)
	(SW)	3 × 4 (80 to 85%)
	Single-arm pullover (Swiss ball)	3 × 6 (using rope)
	Straight-leg deadlift	2 × 6 (75 to 80%)

DAY 2	Conditioning and agility training
	None

DAY 3	Resistance training	
	EXERCISE	**SETS × REPS (% 1RM OR INTENSITY)**
	Abdominal work	Circuit × 2
	Light stretching	5 minutes
	Hang clean to front squat to push press	3 × 4 (75 to 80%)
	Close-grip bench press (SS)	3 × 4 (75 to 80%)
	Lat pull-down (SS) (PW)	3 × 4 to 6 (85 to 90%)
	(SW)	3 × 4 to 6 (80 to 85%)
	Machine leg curl	3 × 4 to 6 (80 to 85%)
	Dumbbell hammer curl (single-leg)	3 × 5 each leg (75 to 80%)

DAY 4	Conditioning and agility training
	None

Week 48   **In-Season**

Take off from all resistance training and extra conditioning during your conference tournament. If your postseason play extends past your conference tournament, you may want to do some resistance training once or twice a week until postseason play is over.

	Resistance training	
	EXERCISE	**SETS × REPS (% 1RM OR INTENSITY)**
DAY 1	Core work	Choose 1 exercise.
	Light stretching	5 minutes
	Dumbbell bench press (CS)	3 × 5 to 6 (75 to 80%)
	Lat pull-down (CS)	3 × 5 to 6 (75 to 80%)
	Leg press (SS)	4 × 10 (65, 75, 75, 75%)
	Hip abduction with band (SS)	3 × 10 each leg
	Romanian deadlift	2 × 5 to 6 (75 to 80%)
	Conditioning and agility training	
DAY 2	None	
	Resistance training	
	EXERCISE	**SETS × REPS (% 1RM OR INTENSITY)**
DAY 3	Abdominal work	3 × 15 to 30
	Light stretching	5 minutes
	Dumbbell incline press (CS)	3 × 5 to 6 (75 to 80%)
	Machine or cable row (CS)	3 × 5 to 6 (75 to 80%)
	Leg extension	3 × 10 (75 to 80%)
	Machine leg curl (CS)	3 × 10 (70 to 75%)
	Back extension (CS)	2 × 15
	Conditioning and agility training	
DAY 4	None	

Recovering Actively: Postseason Workouts

The objective of the postseason, the last four weeks of the training year, is to get back to the basics of physical fitness while allowing your body to recover from the season that just ended. You must give yourself some active rest so that when you do start back with your off-season training you feel refreshed and ready to take your game to the next level. After your last conference tournament game, take some time off from training to give yourself a mental and physical break. If, however, you are continuing championship tournament play you may have to repeat the postseason tournament workout of week 48 (see page 103) to maintain your fitness until the end of your tournament season. If this is the case for you, after your last tournament game, take two weeks off from training, and then go to week 50. If you have any acute (short-term) or chronic (long-term) injuries during this time, take care of those as soon as possible. Do not just think that something small such as a sore joint or a pulled muscle will eventually go away. Make sure the athletic trainer or doctor knows about your injury or nagging pain as soon as possible. What may be a small problem now may become a bigger problem later if not treated.

Resistance Training

Resistance training during your postseason workouts is a time to recover and prepare your body for the type of work that you will be doing in a few weeks when you start your off-season training (see chapter 2). Your resistance training during the postseason does not include free weight training such as those exercises that use barbells and dumbbells or machine exercises such as leg extensions or leg curls. Rather, these weeks are intended to help you learn to control your own body weight by doing sit-ups, push-ups, chin-ups, dips, and inchworms (see chapter 7). These exercises are beneficial for athletes at any age level, but especially for athletes playing at the junior high and high school levels. Learning to lift and control your own body weight is an important prerequisite for younger players before starting a program consisting of free weights or machines. The postseason workout also includes abdominal, lower back, and core work. The 52-week program centers on these three areas year-round because if these areas are strong, you have a better chance of being strong and stable in other areas of the body. Your lower back work consists of back extensions (page 165). This is a great basic exercise to keep the lumbar area strong. Core work can be done by selecting any of the core exercises found on pages 135 through 138.

Photo courtesy of the Charlotte Sting

Charlotte Smith recognizes the need to rest and recover after a long season.

Conditioning

There is no formal conditioning or running during the postseason period. Keep the intensity of exercise to a minimum to prevent burnout and overtraining. You may want to get away from the game of basketball for a while. Weeks 49 through 52 are designed to do just that. You will have a week of complete rest, a week of active rest, and three weeks of physical fitness activities. During this time I suggest not even picking up a basketball. If you follow this suggestion, when you come back for off-season training, you will be hungry for success and more improvement in your game. Conditioning during the postseason phase includes some muscular endurance work such as swimming and jumping rope; these activities provide just enough conditioning to keep your body active and refreshed. Swimming is great for the joints. Swimming should be recreational, however; if you cannot swim well, stay in the shallow end and do the swimming pool workout found in chapter 1. Jump rope work is great for foot quickness. Use your wrist to turn the rope instead of your entire arm and shoulder. Only jump as high as the rope; anything more is wasted energy and leads to slower footwork.Hand-eye coordination work is also included with some juggling of tennis balls or beanbags. Again, no matter what your age, juggling is a great way to improve hand quickness and hand-eye coordination. If you do not know how to juggle, start out by using just two tennis balls or two small beanbags. Learn to juggle these two items with both hands and then just one hand. When you have mastered this exercise, move on to three balls or bags. This must be practiced daily and can be done throughout the entire off-season and preseason.

Week 49 **Postseason**

On Monday through Friday of this week, participate in any "active rest" activity that is not basketball. I recommend swimming, biking, tennis, or golf.

Week 50 **Postseason**

MONDAY	**Active rest**	
	EXERCISE	SETS × REPS (% 1RM OR INTENSITY)
	Juggling	10 minutes
	Light stretching	5 to 10 minutes
	Core work	Choose 1 exercise from pages 135 to 138.
	Push-up	1 × to failure
	Dip	2 × to failure
	Back extension	2 × 10 to 20
	Swimming	10 to 15 minutes
TUESDAY	**Active rest**	
	EXERCISE	SETS × REPS (% 1RM OR INTENSITY)
	Juggling	10 minutes
	Light stretching	5 to 10 minutes
	Chin-up	2 × to failure
	Sit-up	1 × to failure
	Jumping rope	5 to 10 minutes
THURSDAY	**Active rest**	
	EXERCISE	SETS × REPS (% 1RM OR INTENSITY)
	Juggling	10 minutes
	Light stretching	5 to 10 minutes
	Core work	Choose 1 exercise.
	Push-up	1 × to failure
	Dip	2 × to failure
	Back extension	2 × 10 to 20
	Swimming	10 to 15 minutes
FRIDAY	**Active rest**	
	EXERCISE	SETS × REPS (% 1RM OR INTENSITY)
	Juggling	10 minutes
	Light stretching	5 to 10 minutes
	Chin-up	2 × to failure
	Sit-up	1 × to failure
	Jumping rope	5 to 10 minutes

Week 51 **Postseason**

MONDAY

Active rest

EXERCISE	SETS × REPS (% 1RM OR INTENSITY)
Juggling	10 minutes
Light stretching	5 to 10 minutes
Core work	Choose 1 exercise.
Push-up	2 × to failure
Dip	3 × to failure
Back extension	2 × 10 to 20
Swimming	10 to 15 minutes

TUESDAY

Active rest

EXERCISE	SETS × REPS (% 1RM OR INTENSITY)
Juggling	10 minutes
Light stretching	5 to 10 minutes
Chin-up	3 × to failure
Sit-up	2 × to failure
Jumping rope	5 to 10 minutes

THURSDAY

Active rest

EXERCISE	SETS × REPS (% 1RM OR INTENSITY)
Juggling	10 minutes
Light stretching	5 to 10 minutes
Core work	Choose 1 exercise.
Push-up	2 × to failure
Dip	3 × to failure
Back extension	2 × 10 to 20
Swimming	10 to 15 minutes

FRIDAY

Active rest

EXERCISE	SETS × REPS (% 1RM OR INTENSITY)
Juggling	10 minutes
Light stretching	5 to 10 minutes
Chin-up	3 × to failure
Sit-up	2 × to failure
Jumping rope	5 to 10 minutes

Week 52 **Postseason**

	Active rest	
	EXERCISE	**SETS × REPS (% 1RM OR INTENSITY)**
MONDAY	Juggling	10 minutes
	Light stretching	5 to 10 minutes
	Core work	Choose 1 exercise.
	Push-up	3 × to failure
	Dip	3 × to failure
	Back extension	3 × 10 to 15
	Swimming	10 to 15 minutes

	Active rest	
	EXERCISE	**SETS × REPS (% 1RM OR INTENSITY)**
TUESDAY	Juggling	10 minutes
	Light stretching	5 to 10 minutes
	Chin-up	3 × to failure
	Sit-up	3 × to failure
	Jumping rope	5 to 10 minutes

	Active rest	
	EXERCISE	**SETS × REPS (% 1RM OR INTENSITY)**
THURSDAY	Juggling	10 minutes
	Light stretching	5 to 10 minutes
	Core work	Choose 1 exercise.
	Push-up	3 × to failure
	Dip	3 × to failure
	Back extension	3 × 10 to 15
	Swimming	10 to 15 minutes

	Active rest	
	EXERCISE	**SETS × REPS (% 1RM OR INTENSITY)**
FRIDAY	Juggling	10 minutes
	Light stretching	5 to 10 minutes
	Chin-up	3 × to failure
	Sit-up	3 × to failure
	Jumping rope	5 to 10 minutes

Exercises and Drills

The off-season, preseason, in-season and postseason workouts list basketball-specific drills and exercise. Part II details how to do each exercise and drill.

Chapter 6 highlights the benefits of making flexibility work a daily part of your training. Improved flexibility will not only improve your ability to move but will also reduce your risk of injury. The 19 detailed stretches are tailored to improve flexibility for basketball-specific movements. Chapter 7 provides resistance exercises, complex movements, and plyometric drills to help you build your strength and power. The basketball-specific drills in chapter 8 offer ways to include the powerful stop-and-start sprinting, lateral sliding, and explosive jumping—the demands of basketball—into your daily training. Exercises that address fast footwork, balance, and ball-handling skills round out the program in chapter 9. These exercises will help you apply your strength and power gains to your game

Flexibility Exercises

Flexibility is the absolute range of movement in a joint or a series of joints. This tells us that flexibility is not something that is general but is specific to a particular joint or set of joints. So being flexible in one particular area or joint does not mean that you are or will be flexible in another area or joint; being "loose" in your upper body does not mean you are "loose" in your lower body.

A person's flexibility is affected by the following factors:

Internal Factors

- Type of joint (some joints simply are not meant to be flexible)
- Internal resistance within a joint
- Bony structures that limit movement
- Elasticity of muscle tissue
- Elasticity of tendons and ligaments (ligaments do not stretch much and tendons should not stretch at all)
- Elasticity of the skin (skin actually has some degree of elasticity)
- Ability of a muscle to relax and contract to achieve the greatest range of movement

External Factors

- Temperature of the training environment (a warmer temperature is more conducive to increased flexibility)
- Time of day (most people are more flexible in the afternoon than in the morning)
- Stage in the recovery process of a joint, after an injury or after a hard training session
- Age (preadolescents are generally more flexible than adults)
- Gender (females are generally more flexible than males)

- Ability to perform a particular exercise
- Commitment to achieving flexibility

Strength training and flexibility go hand in hand. It is a misconception that there must always be a tradeoff between strength and flexibility. Needless to say, if you neglect your flexibility program to train for strength, you will sacrifice flexibility and vice versa. However, performing exercises for both strength and flexibility need not sacrifice either one. Flexibility training and a good, solid strength program can actually enhance each other.

Muscles around a given joint, however, can become too "loose," or flexible. That is, there can be a tradeoff between flexibility and stability. As you become more limber in a particular joint, the muscles around that joint give it less support. Too much flexibility can be just as bad as not enough because both can increase the risk of injury.

Once a muscle has reached its maximum length, attempting to stretch it even more will only serve to stretch the ligaments and put undue stress on tendons. Ligaments tear when stretched more than 6% of their normal length. Tendons, believe it or not, are not even supposed to be able to lengthen.

Therefore, once you have achieved a desired level of flexibility, use common sense in stretching. You should never feel pain when stretching, only mild tension. The flexibility program that I have designed for this particular program will help basketball players achieve the desired level of flexibility they need to play today's game. In working with NBA and WNBA players for many years, I have seen players who did not stretch enough and suffered chronic injuries, and I have seen players who stretched too much (believe it or not). This program aims to provide the right amount of stretching for optimal fitness.

Types of Flexibility

The different types of flexibility are grouped according to the different types of activities centered on athletic training. Generally, flexibility that involves movement or motion is called *dynamic*. Dynamic flexibility is

Matt Bullard and George Lynch demonstrate the relationship between flexibility and sports performance.

seen in any basketball game as players reach, jump, side step, or quickly change direction.

Flexibility that does not require movement is called *static*. Static flexibility can be active or passive. Static-active flexibility (also called active flexibility) is the ability to assume and maintain extended positions using only the tension of the agonists (the muscle being used or stretched) and the synergists (the muscle used to keep balance and stability in the joint being stretched) while the antagonists are being stretched. An example of this is lifting the leg and keeping it high without any external support other than your own leg muscles.

Static-passive flexibility (also called passive flexibility) is the ability to assume extended positions and maintain them using only your weight, the support of your limbs, or some other apparatus such as a chair. Understand that the ability to maintain the position does not come only from your muscles, as it does with static flexibility. A split is an example of a passive flexibility position.

Research has shown that active flexibility is more closely related to sports achievement than passive flexibility. Active flexibility is more difficult to develop. It also requires muscle strength to be able to hold and maintain a position.

Types of Stretching

Just as there are different types of flexibility, there are also different types of stretching to achieve these types of flexibility. Stretches are either dynamic (with movement) or static (with no movement). Dynamic stretching affects dynamic flexibility, and static stretching affects static flexibility.

The six types of stretching are as follows:

Ballistic. Ballistic stretching uses the movement from a moving muscle or limb in an attempt to force the muscle beyond its normal range of movement. An example is bouncing down repeatedly to touch your toes. This type of stretching can be dangerous for the simple reason that it can injure the muscle being worked. Using this method does not let your muscles adjust to, and relax in, a stretched position. Muscles may even tighten up because they are trying to protect themselves from being pulled. I include ballistic stretching in this list here as a type of stretching *not* to do. It can lead to discomfort and injury of the joints.

Dynamic. Dynamic stretching involves moving parts of the body while gradually increasing reach, speed of the movement, or even both. Note that dynamic and ballistic stretching are not the same! Dynamic stretching involves controlled, gentle movement of the legs and arms within their range of motion, whereas ballistic stretching is done forcefully, going beyond the range of motion. Dynamic stretching does not involve any jerky movements or bouncing. The running warm-ups presented in chapter 1 are a big part of your dynamic stretching program.

Static-active. In a static-active stretch you hold a stretch with no assistance other than the strength of the muscles themselves. An active stretch is difficult to hold. A time of 20 to 30 seconds may be adequate.

Static-passive. In a static-passive, or "relaxed," stretch you assume a position and hold it with some assistance from your own body, a partner, or some other apparatus. An example is bringing your leg up and holding it in place with your hand. Doing a split on the floor is another example of a passive stretch with the floor as the apparatus. This type of stretching is good for cooling down after a hard workout to help reduce muscle fatigue and soreness.

Static. Although many people think that passive and static stretching are the same and use the words interchangeably, the two are quite different. Static stretching involves stretching a muscle or muscle group to its farthest point and then maintaining that position, whereas passive stretching involves a relaxed person (passive) stretching a muscle or muscle group while some external force (again either a person or some apparatus) brings the joint through its full range.

Proprioceptive neuromuscular facilitation (PNF). PNF stretching is currently the fastest, most productive way known to increase overall flexibility. PNF stretching is usually done with a partner to provide resistance; the person being stretched pushes against the partner's resistance for 5 to 15 seconds without movement (this is called an isometric contraction). Seconds later the partner passively takes the joint through its increased range of motion. Many different PNF techniques are available, but the one I have used for years that seems to bring out the best results is the contract-hold and relax. After assuming an initial passive stretch, the person being stretched isometrically contracts the muscle for 5 to 15 seconds, after which the person briefly relaxes the muscle for two to three seconds, and then immediately moves into a passive stretch that stretches the muscle even more than the initial passive stretch. This can be repeated two to three more times, with each stretch lasting 10 to 15 seconds. After the final stretch, the person being stretched relaxes the muscle for 15 to 20 seconds before going to another stretch, or the participant may go directly to another muscle group.

WHAT HAPPENS WHEN YOU STRETCH

The stretching of a muscle fiber starts with what is called the sarcomere—the basic unit of the muscle fiber. As the sarcomere contracts, the area of overlap between the muscle cells increases. Then, as it stretches, this area of overlap decreases, allowing the muscle fiber to elongate, or lengthen. Once the muscle fiber is at its maximum resting length, additional stretching can place force on the surrounding connective tissue. As tension increases, the fibers in the connective tissue align themselves along the same path of force as the tension. So when you stretch, the muscle fiber is pulled out to its full length sarcomere by sarcomere, and then the connective tissue takes up the remaining length. When this happens, it tends to realign any disorganized fibers in the direction of the tension. This realignment helps to rehabilitate scarred tissue back to health so the athlete can resume playing.

When you stretch the muscle, you also stretch an apparatus within the muscle, the muscle spindle. The muscle spindle records the change in muscle length and sends signals to the spine, which receives this information. This starts the stretch reflex, which attempts to resist the change in the muscle length by causing the stretched muscle to contract. The quicker the change in muscle length is, the stronger the muscle contraction will be. This is what "jump training," or plyometrics, is based on. In this way the muscle spindle helps to maintain muscle tone and protect the body from injury.

One reason for holding a stretch for a prolonged length of time is that the muscle spindle becomes used to the new length and starts to reduce its signaling. Over a period of time, you can train your stretch receptors to allow greater lengthening of the muscles. Greater lengthening of the muscle can mean a greater range of movement, which can also mean that more force can be generated when running or jumping. This can translate to a one-inch improvement in the vertical jump or a tenth of a second faster time in running down the court when guarding your man on defense.

Basketball Flexibility Program

If done properly, stretching can do much more than just increase flexibility. It can also do the following:

- Improve physical fitness
- Enhance the ability to learn and perform skilled movements
- Increase mental and physical relaxation
- Reduce the risk of injury to joints, muscles, and tendons
- Reduce muscular soreness
- Reduce the severity of menstruation pain in females

Warming Up

Remember that stretching is not warming up; rather, it is a very important *part* of the warm-up period. A proper warm-up should first raise your body temperature by 1 or 2 degrees Celsius or 1.4 to 2.8 degrees Fahrenheit. It is very important to perform a general warm-up before you stretch. If you perform your stretching before you warm up your muscles, you risk injury during your athletic activities such as basketball. Be sure to do the dynamic warm-up first and the static stretching after that or even wait until after practice to do the static stretching.

The three phases of a good warm-up are as follows:

1. General warm-up
2. Stretching
3. Sport-specific activity

Duration of the Stretch

Many people have different ideas and generally disagree about how long to hold a passive stretch. Many sources tell us that stretches should be held for as little as 10 seconds or as long as 60 seconds. The truth of the matter is that no one really knows for sure the optimal duration to hold a stretch. Many studies suggest 30 to 60 seconds. Although some researchers found that 15 seconds may be sufficient for the hamstrings, we do not know whether 15 seconds is sufficient for other muscle groups. The general consensus is that holding a stretch around 30 seconds is adequate. Children, whose bones are still growing, do not need to hold a passive stretch for an extended time; 7 to 10 seconds should be adequate for them.

Frequency of Stretching

If you really want to improve your flexibility, I suggest stretching at least twice a day—once in the morning and then again in the afternoon (at practice or on your own). For your morning routine, first perform a general warm-up such as riding a stationary bike for 5 to 10 minutes or taking a 5- to 10-minute jog. Then begin your stretching routine with some static stretches, followed by some light dynamic stretches.

Because most people are more flexible in the afternoon or early evening, this can be an ideal time to work on flexibility once again. If you are training in-season, then you are already likely stretching at your practice sessions. If this is not the case, make sure to use this time to get another stretching routine in, even if it is right before you go to bed. It is a great way to relax and unwind from a busy day.

The stretching routine that follows can be used before any game, practice session, or conditioning session. Pick three to five upper body stretches and three to five lower body stretches. Concentrate on the areas that really need improvement. For example, if your hamstrings are particularly tight, spend more time on them. Don't just work on areas in which you are already flexible. Work on the weak links of the body.

You may want to adjust parts of the stretching program to fit the goals you are working on at a certain time. For example, you may choose to do upper body stretching before and after working the chest, back, or shoulders during resistance training. You can perform stretches in a static or dynamic manner. Consider using a jump rope or stretch band for resistance. You can obtain a stretch band from Dick Hartsell, Jump Stretch, 1230 North Meridian, Youngstown, Ohio 44509, 800-344-3539.

Be sure to make time to stretch! There are many positive outcomes from stretching and improving your flexibility, but the most important is the increased playing time on the court you can enjoy as a result of having reduced your chances of injury.

Upper Body

Rear Deltoid

Hold the ends of a band or rope in each hand, extend your arms high, and reach back slightly. You may also rotate at the waist.

Front and Rear Deltoid

The band or rope should go straight down the spine. Your bottom hand should come up as high as possible, and you should feel only mild tension as you pull each end of the band.

Biceps

Hold your arms straight out at each side and rotate your thumbs down so that the palms face the posterior side.

Rotator Cuff (Scarecrow)

With your elbows bent at 90 degrees, stretch the shoulder by pushing the hand toward your back. You have the option of holding both hands in the up position or holding one hand up while the other is down.

Arm Across Chest

This stretches the rear shoulder and upper lats of the back. Keep the arm that is crossing the chest parallel to the floor as you push it against you with your other hand.

Forward and Backward Rotation

Simulate a swimming motion while keeping your arms straight. Bring your hands up and around, both forward and backward. Make sure the rotations are smooth and fluid; there should be no jerky motions.

Lower Body

Knees Side to Side

This stretch is great for warming up the lower back. Lie on your back on the floor with your knees together, and start out with your knees going side to side ever so slightly. As you continue, increase the range of motion until your right leg is touching the right side of the floor and vice versa. Once the leg touches the floor, hold the stretch to each side.

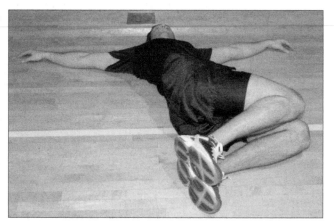

Knee to Chest

You can perform this stretch with one or both knees. It is great for the upper hamstrings and lower back muscles. When performing the one-knee stretch, keep your opposite leg straight and down on the floor while pulling your other knee to your chest. When bringing both knees to your chest, do not rock; hold in a comfortable position.

Groin

This stretch also gets at the adductors of the inner leg. Lie on your back, grab your ankles, and flair your knees out. Push your knees out with your elbows.

Lying Butterfly

You can perform this stretch in a lying or seated position. Keep your heels together and both feet tucked in as close to the groin as possible. Be sure to relax your hips.

Ankle Inversion and Calf

Sit on the floor with legs spread and loop a band once around the ball of your foot. While using resistance from your arm, pull the band so the sole of your foot is pointed outward and hold. Using the same resistance, pull the band so the sole of your foot is pointed inward. While keeping your leg straight, pull the band back slightly, using mild resistance.

Hamstring

Place a band around the ball of your foot (or middle of foot if wearing shoes). Lie on your back on the ground and use mild resistance to pull the leg back. Point your toes down as much as possible to get a great stretch on the calf muscle and hamstrings.

Hip Rotation

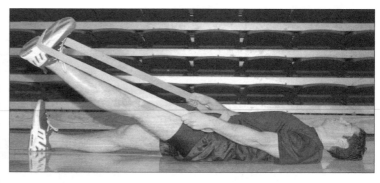

This stretch is effective for loosening and warming up the hip joint and the flexors and extensors that surround the joint. Lying on your back with a band around your foot, make a small circle out to the side in one direction and continuously make the circle bigger. After five to eight circles one way, change direction.

Leg Press

This stretch is effective for working the hamstrings, especially the insertion or bottom part of the muscle. With a band around the ball of your foot (or middle of foot if wearing shoes), lie on your back on the ground and use mild resistance to pull the leg back to a comfortable position. Bend your leg slightly; then press your foot straight up in the air and straighten your leg. Do not hyperextend your knee. Hold the stretch; then repeat the movement by bending your leg and pressing your foot straight up. Hold the stretch. The bending then straightening makes for a good dynamic stretch.

Leg Crossover

Try this stretch to work your lower back and iliotibial (IT) band on the outside of the hip. Lying on your back with the band around the ball of the foot, bring your leg across your body with your opposite leg straight or slightly bent. You may bend and straighten, then again bend and straighten the leg you are crossing over for a dynamic stretch.

Leg to the Side

This stretch is great for the groin, adductors, and abductors. Lying on your back with the band around the ball of your foot (or middle of foot if wearing shoes), hold your leg out to the side at a 30- to 35-degree angle. Pull back slightly for mild resistance. Make sure your opposite leg is straight and on the ground.

Quadriceps

While lying on your side, pull your top foot back toward your buttocks using mild tension and hold. Change sides and repeat with the other leg. You may also bring your knee up and to the side to get a different angle and feel for the stretch.

Quadriceps and Hip Flexor

While lying face down, bend your knee to lift your lower leg back behind you with the band or rope and pull slightly. Lift your hip for an added stretch on the hip flexor.

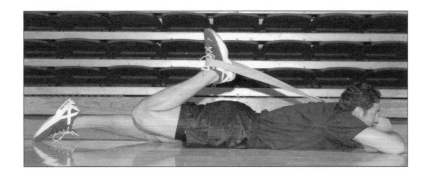

Side Lunge

This stretch is great for stretching the groin area and the adductors of the inner leg. Lunge to the side while balancing on the toes of your bent leg. Make sure you point your toes up on your straight leg to get more stretch in the groin.

Strength and Power Exercises

This chapter covers all training aspects of the strength and power exercises for basketball that are incorporated in this 52-week program. In particular, it covers the basics of overall strength periodization for the program as well as the basics of the contrast training and complex movement lifts that are highlighted in the weekly programs detailed in chapters 2 through 5. In addition, this chapter explains how to perform each resistance training exercise listed in the workouts for the abdominals, core, upper body, and lower body. Finally, it describes the matrix and plyometric workouts that build power.

Every weight room and training facility is different and may include different equipment. For this reason I provide a variety of exercises to choose from. If one piece of equipment is not available, perform another exercise that works the same muscle group. The workouts are designed to be adaptable to your needs, to be fun, and to produce results.

As I stated briefly in chapter 1, in basketball you must be able to perform different unstable movements while still executing the play, shot, or rebound. Balance is the ability to maintain your center of body mass over a base of support without losing control or falling. A continuous chain of muscles in the body helps to maintain a sense of balance and stability. When a disturbance causes your body to lean in a certain direction, the ankles, knees, upper legs, hips, and lower back all act to counteract the instability.

This is where many of the strength and power exercises come in. Creating more instability during a particular lift or movement by standing on one leg, placing one leg on a pad, or even using a Swiss ball can make that chain stronger and lead to positive results on the court. Take advantage of incorporating this training tool into your strength program. You will feel the difference as you build stability!

Strength Periodization

The number of sets and repetitions you perform of any exercise during the various resistance training phases is based on a refined single periodization model (see table 7.1). If you perform 10 to12 repetitions all the time, your body will burn out. Rather, you have to cycle your workout with different exercises, movements, and repetitions to ensure that your training is well rounded. Because different repetitions produce different training results, you should make sure to perform different repetitions of exercises depending on where you are in the training cycle.

Table 7.1 Refined Single Periodization Model

Hypertrophy		Basic strength		Strength and Power	
3 Weeks	2 Weeks	3 Weeks	2 Weeks	2 Weeks	1 Week
4 × 10	3 × 5 to 6	4 × 10	3 × 5 to 6	3 × 3 to 4	3 × 2 to 3

Sets with 10 to 12 repetitions are generally done during the *hypertrophy* phase. This phase prepares you for more intense work. Hypertrophy sets with these higher reps will expand the muscle fiber and give it more short-term endurance, which helps reduce fatigue during later stages of training when the intensity is higher.

Sets with four to six repetitions make up the basic strength phase. These reps are done with explosive but controlled movements. Strength and power phase sets, however, typically use two to three repetitions. During the strength and power phase, the intensity is brought to its highest level. Training at this time is very sport specific, again emphasizing the speed of movement.

Periodize your workouts to achieve maximum strength.

Types of Training

In addition to traditional strength training exercises that focus on particular areas of the body, I also incorporate several other strengthening methods that are specifically suited to basketball. Basketball is a sport combining absolute strength with vertical explosive power, followed by powerful lateral movement. All of this can be done in a very short amount of time, such as going after one rebound. This is why resistance training must simulate and overload these movements. Following is a list of several training methods to use to combine lifts or work in sets to improve basketball skills.

Contrast training is one way to simulate the strength and power of basketball movements. A contrast training exercise might start out with the squat or leg press, and then go right to a power slide or body blade for stability. Another example of a good contrast training exercise is performing an upper body movement such as a bench press, then immediately going to medicine ball throws. Contrast training is a valuable tool to enhance your basketball skills.

Complex training is similar to contrast training except that it involves resistance training with no jumping or lateral work. A complex training set we use is performing a hang clean for five reps, then at the top of the fifth clean movement going into a front squat. After five reps of the front squat, you go directly to a push press for five reps. Again, this increases the intensity of the workload and also increases the metabolic rate of the body, which really burns calories.

Circuit training involves doing three or more different exercises without any (or with very little) rest between exercises. After a 60- to 90-second rest, you repeat the circuit. The circuit can combine absolute strength exercises and explosive movements or separate them. A circuit training workout can be all abdominals, all upper body work, or all lower body work; however, the circuit programs for basketball players ideally include both upper and lower body exercises for a total body workout.

Supersetting is consistently used throughout the 52-week program. You will see an SS noted in many of the workouts. It simply means that after performing one exercise of a particular body part you go directly to the next exercise that works the same body part with very little or no rest in between. In some situations supersetting may be a form of contrast training. Again, the idea is to overload the muscles to build strength and muscular endurance.

Combination movements are much like supersets except that you are training two different body parts instead of similar body parts. When you see CS noted in a workout, it means you should go from one exercise to another with little rest in between.

A **metabolic 3 × 3 workout** is a multijoint hip movement, followed by a multijoint chest exercise, followed by a multijoint upper back movement. I have incorporated this workout into the in-season training because of its short duration (20 to 25 minutes). Once again, you should move as quickly as possible between exercises with 60 to 90 seconds of rest between "trisets." Every set can be trained either short of failure or to complete failure, depending on your schedule of games. You may want to come short of failure if you have a game the day after your 3 × 3 workout. If you have more time to recover, however, (at least three days), a workout to complete failure may be called for.

Matrix workouts take you through three planes of movement rather than one or two as is the case with most resistance exercises. Page 172 covers the two matrix workouts in detail.

Plyometrics are drills aimed at linking strength with speed of movement to produce power. Plyometrics and the training involved are essential to athletes who jump, lift, or run. Pages 172 to 176 cover the basketball-specific plyometrics used in this program.

Tubing exercises use special types of light to heavy tubing to vary the resistance during a movement. Tubing may be used in stretching exercises and can be incorporated with your weight training program. Exercises such as rowing movements for the back and even leg training can help supplement your workout or warm up your body in preparation for the upcoming workout session. Pages 176 to 178 highlight several tubing exercises that are beneficial for basketball players.

Now that we have highlighted several ways to combine lifts to enhance your game, let's cover the basics of each strength exercise.

Some Dos and Don'ts of Resistance Training

Be sure to *do* the following:

- Rotator cuff exercises before all bench press work.
- Light leg extensions before any other leg extensions.
- Breathe correctly when performing each lift—breathe in when lowering the resistance and out during the exertion phase of the lift.

Be sure *not to do* the following:

- Leg extensions in which you straighten the knee completely if you have had knee surgery of any kind (especially ACL surgery). Straightening the knee completely puts too much pressure on the ligaments or tendons that have been repaired.
- Behind-the-neck lat pull-downs, behind-the-neck presses, upright rows, and incline bench presses using a bar. These four exercises put too much strain on the rotator cuff and can cause damage to the area over a long period of time.
- Supine (lying) bench presses with a bar if you have had any type of shoulder surgery. Use a machine or dumbbells instead.

Strengthening the Core

Your resistance training workouts are designed so that you start a workout session with core work (or strengthening your abdominals) 95% of the time. Doing abdominal and core work first warms up the entire body. Moreover, when these two areas are strong, your entire body has a cornerstone from which to build.

A strong abdominal wall helps support and stabilize the entire torso area and even the upper legs. When performing exercises such as hang cleans, squats, or even conditioning, speed drills, or change-of-direction movements, the abdominal wall is a critical factor in strength, speed, and quickness. When the abdominals are strong and functional, other body parts are able to perform more efficiently because of the assistance that the abdominals provide. A balance must exist, however, between the strength of the abdominals and the strength of the lower back. Abdominals that are too strong coupled with a lower back that is too weak can lead to postural problems, altered biomechanics, and other muscle imbalances. Working not only the abdominals but also the entire core area is vital to all-around athletic fitness.

Training the abdominals is different from training the core. Think of the abdominals as the fleshy fruit of the apple and the inner body core as the core of the apple. The core is not the superficial abdominal muscle that you may see at the beach, but the deeper abdominals that help protect and assist the spine and help stabilize movements such as a basketball jump shot or rebound.

Abdominal Exercises

In this chapter I have provided a wide variety of abdominal exercises to choose from. In the abdominal circuit training at the beginning of some of your workouts, pick three different ab exercises and go from one to the other without stopping. For example, you might start with knee raises with straps for 15 reps, go directly to 10 medicine ball side raises, followed directly by 15 upper ab crunches. You might then rest 30 to 45 seconds and repeat the circuit twice more, making sure to rest between circuits.

Knee Raise

Using the straps for this exercise is great for working the lower abdominals. Make sure the straps are tucked up near your armpits. To keep from rocking, bring your hips straight up. Bringing your knees all the way down and then all the way up works the lower abdominals and the hip flexors. To take your hip flexors out of the movement, bring your knees only halfway down and then back up. When straps are not available, use a support bench and place your elbows on the pads.

Medicine Ball Side Raise

Sit on the floor with your back erect, legs spread, and knees slightly bent. Start by holding the ball directly to one side; then bring it directly over your head and down on the other side while keeping your arms as straight as possible. Repeat. Perform two to three sets of 20 reps. Bringing the ball to both sides equals one rep.

Hip-Up

Lie on your back on a bench and bring your knees to your chest; then in one motion drive your hips and legs up in the air as high as possible. Return to the starting position with your legs bent in a 90-degree position and with your lower back flat.

Medicine Ball Sit-Up Throw

Lie on your back on the floor. With your knees bent and driving your heels into the floor, take the medicine ball back until your upper back is flat on the floor. As soon as this happens, drive your upper body up and with one explosive motion throw the medicine ball to your partner, who is three to five yards away (distance condensed in photo). The partner throws the ball back to where your hands are held high and you repeat the motion.

Knees to Chest

Lie flat on your back with your knees bent at a 90-degree angle. Bring your knees to your chest, creating a 15- to 30-degree angle from the floor to your lower back. Keep two to three fingers behind each ear throughout the movement. Be sure to initiate the movement with your lower abdominals by keeping them tight during the entire set. Also try to keep your lower back flat during this exercise. This discourages the contraction of other muscle groups and puts the tension directly on the lower abs.

Side Crunch

Lie on your back with your feet on the ground and your knees bent. Place one arm straight out to the side; bend the other arm, placing two or three fingers behind the ear. When coming up, keep your bent elbow back and bring your shoulder slightly across your body in line with the opposite hip joint. Your range of motion will be short. Repeat on other side.

Upper Ab Crunch

Lying on your back, start with your legs up and bent at 90 degrees. Keep your lower back flat throughout the exercise. Put each hand on the side of your temple with your elbows in. Bring your upper back off the floor, with your chest going straight up. You may hold a 5- to 10-pound weight behind your head for added resistance.

Note that the previous three exercise are great exercises to do in a tri-set manner.

Rugby Sit-Up

Lie on your back on the floor. Keep your lower back flat throughout the movement of this modified sit-up. As you bring your left knee in, your right elbow comes across your body to meet it. When your right knee comes in, your left elbow comes across.

Regulation Sit-Up

This type of sit-up is used primarily for testing purposes and during the postseason. Lie on your back on the floor and bend your knees at about 90 degrees, with your heels on the floor and your fingers on your temples or behind your ears. When you have raised up such that your elbow joint is in line with your knee joint, you may go down to the starting position (with your upper back flat on the floor). No one should hold your feet down while you perform this movement because this works the hip flexors much more than the abdominal wall.

Core Exercises

I provide seven core exercises to choose from that are fun but challenging. Remember when training the core to stay in a neutral position; that means no hyperextension and no flexion of the hips. Keep the abdominals and external obliques tight throughout the movement of all core training. Select one or two drills for each of your designated workout sessions.

Inchworm

This exercise is great not only for working the abdominals but also for stretching the lower back, hamstrings, and calves. Start in a push-up position and keep your legs straight at all times. Slowly work your feet toward your hands by taking small steps on your toes. While doing this, be sure not to move your hands. When your hips are as high as possible and you cannot move your feet forward, move your hands up as far as possible to the push-up position, keep your entire body as straight as possible, and then repeat. Try to go 15 to 20 yards; then turn around and come back. You may work up to 20 to even 30 yards and back.

Medicine Ball Hold on Swiss Ball

Sit up straight on a Swiss ball while squeezing your lower abdominals. While holding the medicine ball as high as possible, have your partner or coach push on the medicine ball or any part of your upper body for five to six seconds. The partner or coach then releases and pushes again in another direction and on another part of your body or medicine ball. Repeat this four to five times. Make sure when sitting on the ball that you keep your feet flat on the floor and no greater than shoulder-width apart.

Standing Swiss Ball Hug

Stand with your feet shoulder-width apart, maintaining an athletic position with knees slightly bent throughout this exercise. While hugging the ball and keeping your lower abdominals tight, have your partner push the ball for one to four seconds in one direction and then repeat in another direction. Total time should be 30 seconds in multiple directions. Perform three sets of 30 seconds.

Swiss Ball Bridge

While lying on your back with a Swiss ball between your shoulder blades and your hips up and in a neutral position, have your partner or coach push on different areas of your body such as your hips, legs, and shoulders. Be sure to keep your legs at 90 degrees and feet shoulder-width apart. As your partner pushes, hold your entire body in position as you feel resistance. Do not move; try to stay as still as possible. Each resistance from your partner should be around four to six seconds. While your partner pushes, squeeze your lower abdominals. Perform two to three sets of five to six pushes.

Medicine Ball Throw on Swiss Ball

Position your upper back on a Swiss ball. Keep your lower back and hips parallel to the floor while your partner tosses a medicine ball so it drops outside your center of gravity. Your partner should toss it to the right or left of your chest. As you throw the medicine ball back, you may roll onto your lower back. Keep your feet shoulder-width apart to help you brace and balance while catching and throwing the medicine ball.

Jackknife

Assume a push-up position with your shins on top of a Swiss ball, keeping your body in a straight line from head to toe. Start by pulling the ball up toward your torso by drawing your knees to your chest. Keep your lower abs and core strong and tight as you bring the ball in and extend your legs back to the starting position. Perform three sets of 10 reps.

Russian Twist

While sitting and leaning back on a Swiss ball, hold a medicine ball out in front of you with your arms extended out and only slightly bent. Keep your knees no wider than shoulder-width apart. Move the ball side to side by rotating your torso. When going from side to side, keep the medicine ball in a 10 o'clock to 2 o'clock range. Keep your lower abs and core tight and strong throughout the range of movement. Perform three sets of 20, with going from side to side being one rep. You may also perform these twists while sitting on some type of pad to create instability (as in the photos). You may also try doing a set bringing the medicine ball in to your chest.

Chest Exercises

The chest exercises presented here build absolute strength and explosive power and emphasize functional strengthening for basketball. Many of these are used in the contrast or combo sets as well as the circuits.

Floor Bench Press

Lie on your back with your lower back flat on the floor and your legs bent. You may want to have a spotter on each side of the bar to help lift the bar up to the starting position and to take the weight back to the floor when you are finished. When you are bringing the weight down to the chest area, make sure to control the weight and use a soft touch when your elbows hit the floor. As soon as this happens, extend your arms up to finish the lift.

Dip

When doing conventional dips (weighted or unweighted) using a dip stand, lean slightly forward. The descent should be slow and under control. When your elbow angle gets to 90 degrees, return to the starting position. Women may have someone hold their ankles and feet to assist during the movement. Other variations of dips work the shoulders (see scapular dip) and triceps (see reverse triceps push-up).

Dumbbell Bench Press

Position your upper back on top of a Swiss ball with your hips up and in a neutral position. Place your feet no wider than shoulder-width apart. Start with the dumbbells fully extended upward. Slowly bring them down. When you feel a slight stretch in your chest area, return to the starting position.

Dumbbell Incline Press

Position your back on the ball just as for the bench press. Keep your hips down and chest out throughout the movement. With your arms extended upward, bring the dumbbells down slowly and with control until you feel a slight stretch in your upper chest. Then lift the weight upward to the starting position.

Swiss Ball Walkout Push-Up

Position your abdomen on top of the ball. Roll forward and walk out on your hands until your ankles and shins are on top of the ball; then start your push-up. When finished, walk back to the starting position. Keep your core tight throughout the entire movement. Women may put their knees on the ball instead of their ankles to assist in the movement. Be sure to keep your hips down in a neutral position, with no extension or flexion of the hips.

Basketball Push-Up

Place a basketball under each hand and perform a push-up. Spread your hands and squeeze the balls as hard as possible throughout the pushup.

Swiss Ball Balance Push-Up

Position your abdomen on top of the ball. Roll forward and walk out on your hands until your ankles and shins are on top of the ball. Position your hands on a balance board and begin your push-ups. Keep your core and lower abdominals tight throughout the entire movement.

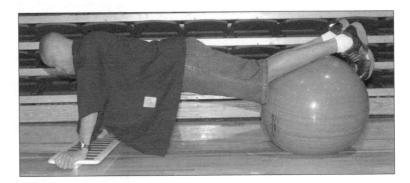

Medicine Ball Chest Pass

Position both knees on a pad. With your upper body erect and your chest out, push the medicine ball out in an explosive manner to your partner, who is standing five to six yards (distance condensed in photo) away. When performing the chest pass, try to push out with both hands evenly; do not use more force with your dominant hand.

Medicine Ball Pullover and Throw

This exercise involves the same movement as the dumbbell pullover. Start with your upper back on a flat bench or Swiss ball. For this particular exercise keep your hips down (to get a good stretch in the chest and upper torso area) and your feet shoulder-width apart. Throw the medicine ball with a two-arm explosive overhead throw to a partner who is standing five to seven yards away. Your partner should throw the ball back slightly over your head so that the pullover is only two motions (catch or pull and throw).

Dumbbell Fly

Place your upper back on the end of the bench with your hips down. Start with your arms extended straight overhead. When taking the dumbbells down, bend your arms slightly. When you feel a good stretch in your chest area, bring the dumbbells back up as if you were putting your arms around a big tree trunk. You can also perform the fly on a machine.

Rotator Cuff Exercises

These exercises help keep the rotator cuff muscles strong, healthy, and balanced. The rotator cuff is made up of four muscles: the infraspinatus, teres minor, supraspinatus, and the subscapularis. Although these four muscles have different roles and functions, they act as one unit to achieve one common goal—to stabilize the shoulder joint. Without this stability, the larger muscles that move the shoulder and arm cannot perform properly, no matter how strong or healthy they seem to be.

When a particular training day calls for rotator cuff exercises, choose one or two exercises from those described here. Perform two to three sets of 8 to 10 reps for each exercise.

Band Work

Stand erect and keep your elbows tucked in to the side of your torso throughout both movements. Internal rotation occurs when you bring the band in to your chest. External rotation occurs when you take the band out to the side of your torso, again keeping your elbows tucked into the side of your upper body.

Scapular Dip

Sit on a bench with hands on both sides of the body gripping the edge of the bench. Lift yourself off the bench with your arms, straightening your arms and your legs, and planting your heels on the floor. Slowly lower your body by bending your elbows 10 to 15 degrees. Use your upper back muscles to initiate the dip. Straighten your arms to come back up.

Prone Row External Rotation

Start by placing your midchest on top of the Swiss ball with your feet on the floor and shoulder-width apart. With your arms hanging down under your shoulders, lift your elbows directly up. A view from the top should show that your elbows are parallel with each other and your upper back at this point. Next, externally rotate your arms until they are horizontal to the ground, keeping your elbows at 90 degrees throughout the range of motion. Hold the dumbbells up for a count, then derotate, moving your arms back down to the initial starting position, and repeat.

Supraspinatus Fly

This exercise is also called the "empty can." Stand erect with hands at your sides and hold a 2.5- to 8-pound dumbbell in each hand with thumbs pointing down (arms rotated inward). Keeping your arms straight, raise them forward and slightly out to each side until both dumbbells are at eye level. Hold for a count of 5 to 10, and then return to the starting position. Keep both arms straight throughout the entire movement.

Scarecrow

Stand with a 5- to 10-pound dumbbell in each hand and hold both arms straight out at shoulder height. Bend each elbow to 90 degrees so that both hands are pointing downward. Then rotate both arms upward, maintaining the 90-degree angle at the elbows.

Shoulder Extension

Stand with your knees bent slightly and your upper body leaning over until it is parallel to the floor. Using dumbbells that are 2.5 to 8 pounds, bring your arms straight back with your thumbs out and your palms facing down. Lift your arms until they are parallel to the floor, and then return to the starting position.

Internal Rotation

Lie on your side with a 2.5- to 10-pound dumbbell in your down hand. Keeping that arm bent at a 90-degree angle, rotate it inward to the upper abdominal area, and then return to the starting position.

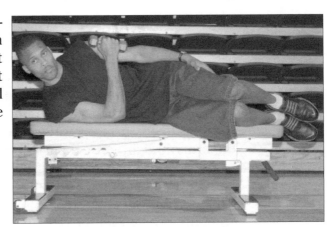

External Rotation

Lie on your side with a 2.5- to 10-pound dumbbell in your upper hand. Again, keeping that arm bent at a 90-degree angle, rotate it upward. Remember to face your palm inward when your hand is in the down position and outward when in the upward position. Keep your elbow tucked into your hip during the entire exercise.

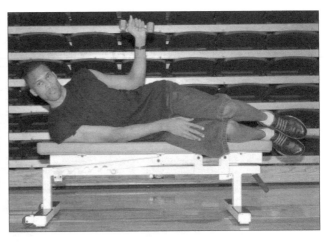

Arm Exercises

The weight training exercises I have chosen for arm work are for both absolute strength and sport-specific application. The dumbbell hammer curls and the reverse curls are for forearm work, which is an important factor in rebounding or just making sure that no one is able to take the ball out of your hands. The other biceps and triceps work is to help you gain the absolute strength and muscular endurance that is important when you are fighting for position under the boards or making sure your jump shot is still strong in the last half of the game.

Dumbbell Hammer Curl

You can perform this exercise while seated on a bench, standing on both legs, or standing on one leg. You may alternate each hammer curl or lift each dumbbell at the same time during the exercise. Make sure your thumbs are pointed up and your elbows are kept in close to your body during the entire movement.

Reverse Triceps Push-Up

Start by facing away from the bench with your hands braced on the edge of the bench and your feet up on another bench. With your legs slightly bent, lower your body in a slow and controlled descent. When your arms are bent at a 90-degree angle, or just below that point, return to the starting position with your triceps in full extension. For added resistance, put a weight in a comfortable position in your lap.

Biceps Curl

You can perform the biceps curl using dumbbells (alternating or together), a barbell, or a machine. When using free weights, stand with your feet together and arms extended (dumbbells by your side, barbell resting on your thighs). Begin the lift with your palms facing away and up during the movement. When you reach a full contraction at the top, return to the starting position.

Reverse Arm Curl

This exercise is very similar to the biceps curl except that you use a reverse grip (palms down). Keep your elbows in close to your body during the entire movement.

Triceps Cable Push-Down

Grasp a bar attached to a high cable. Start with the forearms parallel to the floor to make a 90-degree angle with the elbow. Keep both elbows tightly tucked to the sides and slightly in front of the body. Extend the forearms downward to full extension. Return to the starting position to complete the movement.

Dumbbell Triceps Kickback

While holding a dumbbell in each hand, bend over at the hips with the knees bent slightly. Your upper back should be almost parallel to the floor. Extend the lower arms straight back so that they are in line with the upper arms. The arms at this point should be almost even or parallel with the floor or the upper back. Do not use the shoulders to assist in the movement. Work only the lower arm from the wrist to the elbow so that the triceps will be isolated. You can also perform this exercise using one arm at a time. Simply use the other arm to support the upper body by placing it on a bench or chair.

Dumbbell Triceps Extension

Avoid using heavy weight on this exercise to keep from putting too much stress on the triceps tendons. When performing this movement with a single arm, extend a dumbbell straight over your head. Take the dumbbell down as if you were going to touch or scratch the middle of your back with it, then bring it up to the starting position. Keep your elbow pointed straight up toward the ceiling during the entire movement. You can also perform the movement using both hands to grip one dumbbell. Make sure you keep both elbows pointed up during the exercise. This exercise can be performed standing or seated.

Leg Exercises

Nothing feels worse than losing your leg strength during a game. Working your legs with weight resistance exercises can greatly benefit your game in running, change of direction, and rebounding. It can also help in producing the explosive strength you need to play today's game. I have chosen a variety of leg movements that will aid greatly in the areas I have just mentioned and in other areas that are critical in taking your game to another level.

Front Squat

The front squat helps you keep your upper body erect when performing any type of squat variation. It is also great for strengthening the core; because of the position of the bar resting on the front shoulders, the upper quadriceps really get a workout. When jumping during a game, you bend at the knees, not the lower back, and the front squat helps you do just that and obtain good jump mechanics.

Start by setting the bar high on the shoulders with a grip that is shoulder-width apart. Point your elbows directly at the wall in front of you and keep your upper body erect during the entire movement. You need good wrist flexibility when doing front squats. You may have problems at first keeping your elbows up; however don't give up—you'll keep improving each time.

Straight-Leg or Romanian Deadlift

The legs are kept straight throughout the straight-leg deadlift to isolate the hamstrings. During the Romanian deadlift, which works the lower back as well as the hamstrings, the legs bend. When first starting the deadlift, use lighter weights to minimize the stress on the lower back. Start out by holding the bar using an overhand shoulder-width grip. The bar should be in front of the legs.

Begin the movement by standing erect; take the bar straight down until you feel a slight stretch in the hamstrings, then bring the bar up to a standing position. As you become accustomed to the lift you may take the bar down lower each time. Keep the bar close to your body during the entire movement.

Single-Leg Squat

This is one of my favorite exercises because it makes you stay upright, meaning that your upper torso must be erect. This can be done on a Smith machine, usually used in-season, or using free weights. The foot of your back leg is hooked over a bench while your upper leg takes the workload. Make sure that you sit back on your hips until the bottom of your hamstring is parallel with the floor. Your squatting knee should not pass in front of your front foot when squatting.

Box Squat

When performing box squats, use the same form as with regular squats. Select the right size box; when you sit down on it, the bottom of your hamstring should be parallel to the floor. Keep your lower back tight and your chest big and wide when you sit back, and bring the hips back as far as possible. When coming up off the box, keep all the pressure on your heels and midfoot. Squeeze the lower abdominals to ensure stability and to aid in the upward movement. Do not get into a rocking motion when sitting back and coming up.

Side Squat

Throughout the side squat, position your feet five to six inches wider than your shoulders. Place the bar high on the trapezius and point your toes straight ahead. From the standing position, squat to one side or the other. Make sure when squatting laterally that you drive your hips back during the eccentric phase of the lift while keeping your torso erect. The opposite leg should remain almost straight during the entire movement.

Leg Extension

Before beginning resistance work with the legs, I always have athletes warm up the knee joints and quadriceps with leg extensions. This is a great way to get any stiffness out of the joint and to stabilize the knee and the surrounding area. Never lift too heavy a weight on leg extensions (use light to medium weight) because this can lead to quadriceps or patellar tendinitis.When performing leg extensions, women in particular need to keep the toes pointed out and the pads on the inside of the ankles to help strengthen and develop the vastus medialis muscle (located inside the upper leg).

Leg Press

Women who perform the squat or leg press also need to keep their toes pointed straight ahead. Because women have wider hips than men have, they may have a tendency to rotate the upper leg inward when performing these two movements. You can help correct this by keeping the toes pointed straight and also keeping the knees directly over the second and third toes.

Dumbbell Leg Curl

Using a bench: Have a partner place the dumbbell between your feet. Use your legs to lift the dumbbell toward your buttocks, then extend your legs to a straight position. Make sure you keep pressing the ankles together during the entire movement to keep the dumbbell from falling and to maintain control during the exercise.

Using a Swiss ball: Align your waist on top of the ball with your hand on the floor to help control and balance the movement of the leg curl.

Swiss Ball Leg Curl

With the bottom of your calf muscle and ankle on top of the ball, raise your hips in a bridge position. Bend the knees to 90 degrees, rolling the ball with your feet up and then extend your legs back to the starting position.

Machine Leg Curl

Position yourself and move just as in the dumbbell leg curl, but lift machine weights rather than a dumbbell.

Body Blade

The body blade is a great tool for creating instability and activating the stabilizer muscles. One way to do so is to stand on one leg and perform a half to a quarter squat. The opposite knee should be up and bent. Shake the blade with one or two hands to help create instability at the ankle, knee, and hip area. Perform for 15 to 20 seconds; then switch legs. The down leg should be kept slightly flexed during the entire movement.

Hip Abduction

Place a Thera-Band around both ankles and position your feet shoulder-width apart. Raise one leg out to the side and back while keeping the other leg slightly bent. To create instability, do not hold onto any fixed piece of equipment. Start by holding your hands out to help with balance; as you become more comfortable with the movement, place your hands on your hips.

Walking Lunge

You can perform walking lunges using a bar or medicine ball. Either way, keep your upper torso erect, with your chest wide and your lower back arched. When lunging, do not let your knee go out over your foot. Press off midfoot to heel when coming up. Hold the medicine ball or bar straight out with your arms fully extended. When the right leg lunges forward, turn and rotate the medicine ball, chest, and head to the left. When the left leg lunges forward, turn and rotate to the right. You may also try pressing the ball upward and out with no rotation of the upper body.

Side Lunge

The side lunge is much like the side squat, but in this movement you start with your feet directly under you. Step out directly to the side with your right foot as far as comfortable. Keeping your left foot planted and your left knee straight, bend your right leg while moving your hips laterally to the right. Make sure you sit back while moving to the side to avoid positioning your knees over your toes. Keep your shoulders square and your toes straight throughout the movement.

Side Step-Up

Use a box 12 to 14 inches high and 18 to 24 inches wide. Stand beside the box holding dumbbells down by your side. Using the leg nearest the box, step up and across, attempting to reach the far side of the box. Continue the movement until both feet are up on the box, and then step back down laterally off the same side of the box. Keep your shoulders square throughout the exercise. Once finished, repeat the movement on the other side.

Crossover Side Step-Up

Use the same box that you use for the side step-up. Holding a pair of dumbbells down by your side and with your right leg nearest the box, cross your left leg over your right until you have stepped all the way up on the box. Continue the lateral movement until both feet are up on the box. When stepping down, start with your left foot, then your right, and then repeat the movement for all of the prescribed reps. When finished, repeat the drill on the other side.

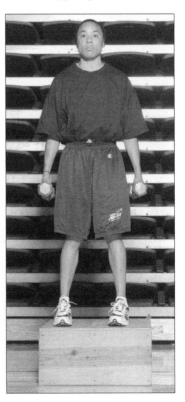

Bench Step-Up

This exercise is done a little differently from the regular step-up. First, place one leg on the bench so that it is bent at a 90-degree angle to the other leg. With the leg on the bench, press up so that the leg is fully extended and you are up on your toes. At the same time raise the lower leg up high with your knee bent. As soon as you touch the floor on the way down, explode back up. You may add intensity by pressing dumbbells overhead at the top of the movement.

Power Slide

With the weighted bar on your back and a Thera-Band around your ankles, assume an athletic position with your knees bent and your chest wide and big. Squat down and power slide to the right for four to six steps; then power slide to the starting position. Remember to stay low and keep your shoulders square.

Heel Raise

You can perform heel raises using a calf machine, or if you don't have access to a calf machine, by putting a dumbbell in one hand and stabilizing yourself with the other while you stand on one leg. Make sure you rise as high as possible on the toes when performing this movement and bend the knees only slightly to isolate the gastrocnemius (calf muscle). This muscle contributes greatly to running and jumping. The seated calf machine works a similar calf muscle called the soleus that has the same function as the gastrocnemius.

Shoulder Exercises

Your shoulder is the most flexible joint in your body, allowing you to throw a long pass down court, lift a heavy weight, or scratch your back. Your shoulder joints allow you to reach in almost any direction. This joint is like a ball in a small, shallow saucer. The ball, or head of the arm bone called the humerus, rests in the shoulder socket, which is called the glenoid. Small muscles and other parts of the joint called stabilizers help to hold the humeral head and the glenoid together to keep the joint stable.

Because of the importance of the shoulder joint (also called the shoulder complex), you must keep this body part strong, healthy, and flexible. When you jump, the shoulder plays a critical part in the explosiveness that sends you upward. When you're running down court, your shoulders help your legs create acceleration, and when you rebound, your shoulders help you grab and hold the ball.

The shoulder exercises included in this section can aid in your overall improvement and help prevent any serious injury that may occur because of the physical nature of the game. I also include some shoulder exercises with a balance component. Balance is the cornerstone to being a good athlete. Players without good, controlled balance and stability cannot be as effective on the court as they need to be! For this I have included some single-leg exercises. After just a few training sessions, you'll feel and see an improvement in your balance and stability.

Push Press

This exercise can be done with two dumbbells or a barbell gripped just outside a shoulder-width. Start by lowering into a quarter squat position, and then explode upward by pressing the dumbbells (or barbell) with your arms into full extension. Be sure to come up on your toes at the top of the movement.

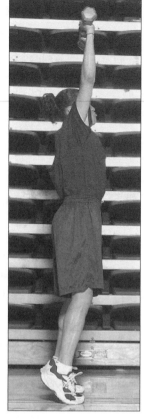

Swiss Ball Floor Press

Start with your abdominals on top of the ball. Roll out until your knees are on top of the ball and your hands are on the floor a little wider than shoulder-width apart. Bring your chin down until it is almost touching the floor; then press back up to the starting position. Keep your abdominals tight throughout the movement.

Single-Leg Dumbbell Press

This exercise is excellent for balance and stability work. Perform a dumbbell press while standing on one leg on a stability pad. Be sure to keep the down leg slightly flexed and the lower abdominals tight throughout this or any other single-leg movement.

Dumbbell Side Raise

Again, you can increase the conditioning effect of the dumbbell raise by performing it while standing on one leg on an unstable surface such as a stability pad.

Dumbbell Push-Up, Press, and Twist

While holding a dumbbell in each hand, assume a push-up position. Take one dumbbell off the ground and hold it against your side while pressing up and fully extending the other arm. Then extend the dumbbell at your side straight up. Keep your eyes on the dumbbell that is being pressed throughout the exercise. You may alternate sides with each repetition or do the recommended reps and then go to the other side.

Dumbbell Front Shoulder Raise

You may alternate or lift both at the same time. Begin with the at your sides, then raise each so that both arms are parallel Return to the starting position, your thumbs up during the entire This exercise can also be done ing on one leg.

Close-Grip Bench Press

Start with your grip just inside shoulder width. Keep your elbows in by your sides during the entire movement. Bring the bar down three quarters of the way; then extend the bar back up to the starting position.

Dumbbell Rear Shoulder Raise

Lean over with your upper back parallel to the floor and your knees slightly bent. Start with the dumbbells hanging down directly under your chest. Take the dumbbells out to the side and up, with your arms slightly bent. Keep your upper arms parallel to the floor; then return to the starting position. You can also perform this exercise while lying over a Swiss ball.

Seated Row Press

This exercise works the upper back and is usually performed on a seated row machine. Sit up straight, keeping the knees slightly bent throughout the movement to reduce pressure on the lower back. Grasp the bar with both hands and pull it to the rib cage, squeezing the shoulder blades together. On the eccentric contraction (when the bar is going away from the body), bend forward only slightly.

Military Press

Begin by gripping the bar while it is positioned in the rack with a shoulder-width grip. While holding the bar at the upper chest level, step back from the rack and press the bar straight up as high as possible, then down to the starting position. Do not use the hips and legs during the concentric phase of the lift or the pushing up of the bar.

Upper Back Exercises

These exercises work the section of the upper back from the lower cervical spine through the entire thoracic spine. The muscles involved include the following:

Trapezius—the flat triangular muscle of the upper back and shoulder that acts to help rotate the scapula, raise the shoulder, and abduct and flex the arm.

Rhomboids—the muscles of the upper back that help stabilize the scapula while drawing it toward the spine and upward.

Latissimus dorsi—one of a pair of large triangular muscles on the thoracic and lumbar areas of the back. It extends, adducts, and rotates the arm medially; draws the shoulder down and back; and draws the body up.

In simple terms, these muscles play a vital role in helping to stabilize your upper body when you are going up for a jump shot or providing the needed strength when you are pulling down a rebound. They also help support the movement and function of the chest muscles. The exercises in this section serve the specific functions just listed while adding much-needed upper body strength and power.

Lat Pull-Down

Change your grip from workout to workout or from set to set, from wide grip, to close grip, to reverse grip. Pull the bar down to your upper chest.

Swiss Ball Lat Pull-Down

Sit directly on top of the ball with your feet flat on the ground and shoulder-width apart. Keep your upper torso erect and your abdominal area tight. With an underhand or overhand grip, pull the cable down to your side, keeping your elbow in line with your shoulder and wrist. While reaching up and at the top of the pull, keep the abdominals tight and the feet on the floor or box to help with stability.

Swiss Ball Chin-Up

You may use a Smith machine for your chin-up bar. This enables you to select different starting heights. You can also choose an over- or underhand grip. Put your ankles or heels on top of a Swiss ball, and keep your legs straight. Balance the ball with your feet and legs. Keep your hips up throughout the movement.

Chin-Up

If you need assistance during your chin-ups, have a partner hold your feet and the bottom of your lower leg. Keep your chest out and your shoulders back during the exercise. You may choose your grip or even change grips from set to set. For one set you may do a conventional chin-up (palms facing away), and then for the next set you may do a pull-up grip with palms facing toward you. The latter grip puts more workload on your biceps and less on your back.

Power Shrug

Start by standing erect with your grip just outside your upper legs. Bring a bar (or two dumbbells) down two to four inches above your knees. When doing this, bring your hips back out, arch your lower back, and expand your chest. When lowering the bar, do not slide it down your legs. To avoid doing this, keep your shoulders slightly out over the bar. When the bar is two to four inches from your knees, immediately drive your shoulders straight up as though you were going to touch your earlobe. As you move upward, extend your legs and hips, and come up on your toes as high as possible. Do not use your arms to lift the weight; keep them straight during the entire movement. When you reach the highest point, come back down to the starting position, get set, and repeat the exercise.

Hang Clean

This exercise is similar to the power shrug except that, when driving the bar up, you pull it to your upper chest, keeping your elbows higher than your wrists throughout the lift. When the bar has reached your upper chest, flip your wrists under and bring your elbows around until they are pointing straight ahead. As you increase the weight, you will have to squat lower to get your chest under the bar. Your front squats will help prepare you for racking or holding the weight at the end of the movement. It may take a while to get used to pointing the elbows straight ahead toward the wall, but be patient; your wrist flexibility will improve!

Dumbbell Pullover

Lying on your back on a bench, hold a dumbbell with both hands and extend your arms over your head. Use a six-second count to bring the dumbbell forward to your abdomen. Use a four-second count to move it back to the starting position.

Machine or Cable Row

When performing machine or cable rows, sit up with the upper torso erect and pull the bar or cable toward the lower part of the front of the rib cage. Force the shoulders back and the chest out while forcing out the air on the concentric contraction or when you are pulling the bar or cable in toward the body. Be sure to squeeze the shoulder blades together to create a better contraction of the upper back.

Single-Arm Pullover

In this partner exercise you use a Swiss ball and a jump rope. Place your upper back on top of the ball with your hips up and your feet shoulder-width apart. Grab one end of a jump rope or other heavy rope with your right hand. Your partner holds the other end while standing behind the ball. With your partner giving resistance on the rope, take the rope from high above your right shoulder across your body to your left hip and come back to the starting position the same way. Moving the rope from the shoulder to the hip should take around six seconds. Coming back to the starting position, from hip to shoulder, should take around four seconds. After the prescribed reps, switch to the other arm.

Lower Back Exercises

The lower back region is called the lumbar area, named after the lumbar portion of the spinal column. It has five large bones called vertebrae that attach at the base of the spine to a bone called the sacrum, which attaches to the remainder of the bony pelvic ring.

During my tenure as a strength coach with the NBA and the WNBA, players periodically experienced lower back problems. Most of the time these injuries, either big or small, could have been prevented if the player had focused on doing some lower back exercises at least two days a week. The lower back exercises listed here can help strengthen and stabilize the area and in most cases help prevent an injury that may occur down the road.

A strong and stable lower back is an important part of the core; along with the abdominals, it facilitates the body's overall function and movement. Particularly in basketball, lower back strength is important, whether you're fighting under the boards for a rebound or quickly changing direction during a fast transition game.

Back Extension

When doing back extensions, place the pad just below your waist. Keep your head in a neutral position, with your hands on your temples throughout the movement. When coming up, your upper body should be parallel to the floor.

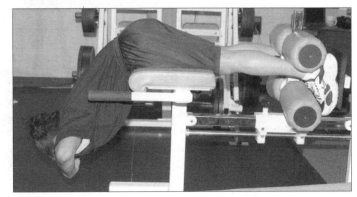

Reverse Hyperextension

If you do this exercise on a bench with a medicine ball, have the support pad slightly above your waist. With your feet together, tap the floor with your toes and then bring both feet up as high as possible. For added resistance hold a three- to five-pound medicine ball between your feet. Remember to keep your head in a neutral position. Contract the core throughout the movement.

To do this exercise on a Swiss ball, lie over the

ball in a prone position and grasp the bar on the Smith machine. Extending your legs with your feet together, bring your ankles, knees, and hips up to a comfortable extension and then back down until your toes tap the floor. Again, squeeze the core throughout the movement with your head in a neutral position.

Good Morning

Place the bar high on your upper feet should be shoulder-width your legs should be slightly back is upright in the starting As you bring the bar down, keep back arched and your hips out throughout the entire move-

Medicine Ball Exer-

Your medicine ball work con- explosive movements that are and specific to basketball. The

back. Your

the medicine ball you use should depend on your strength level. Choose a medicine ball that you can control but that gives the resistance and intensity needed to help you make the improvements and gains you desire.

I have included seven medicine ball drills for you to choose from. In addition to those listed here, see also the medicine ball side raise (page 132), medicine ball sit-up throw (page 133), medicine ball hold on Swiss ball (page 135), medicine ball throw on Swiss ball (page 136), Russian twist (page 137), medicine ball chest pass (page 140), and medicine ball pullover and throw (page 141).

Single-Leg Medicine Ball Throw

Stand on one leg. Use a chest pass to throw the medicine ball to a partner. The partner then returns the ball. Catch the ball at the chest. To increase the degree of difficulty, you may also stand on some type of pad (Airex) while you throw and catch.

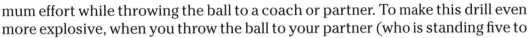

Kneeling Medicine Ball Chest Pass

Kneel with both knees on a pad, with your upper body erect and your chest big and wide. Use equal force with both hands and maximum effort while throwing the ball to a coach or partner. To make this drill even more explosive, when you throw the ball to your partner (who is standing five to

seven yards away), immediately drop your hands down to the floor (staying on your knees) to do a push-up, then explode back up to catch the ball at chest level. Repeat quickly 5 to 10 times.

Power Slide Chest Pass

Use an 8- to 12-pound medicine ball. Face a partner who is standing five to seven yards away (distance condensed in photo). Perform power slides while throwing chest passes. Stay low with your chest out and knees bent. Power sliding from baseline to half court and back equals one set.

Medicine Ball Backboard Toss

Perform a two-hand pass to throw a medicine ball up against the backboard, jumping up as high as possible and extending your arms fully. After catching the ball, immediately go down into a quarter squat position; then explode back up into your two-hand pass.

Medicine Ball Wall Throw

Stand three to five yards (distance condensed in photo) from the wall and perform two-hand side rotation passes, alternating sides. To isolate the core, when going to the right side, bring the ball back only to the 2 o'clock position and then explode the ball out. When the ball goes to the left side, bring the ball back only to the 10 o'clock position and then explode the ball out against the wall. Keep your hips in a neutral position throughout the movement—that is, limit the flexion and extension of your hips throughout the exercise.

Medicine Ball Squat Press

Start by holding the medicine ball with both hands at chest level. Go down in a squat position with your chest and hips back. When you hit a quarter squat position, explode up and immediately throw the medicine ball up as high as possible from a two-hand chest pass position. When going upward, be sure once again to extend your legs and arms as high as possible.

Medicine Ball Squat Throw

This exercise is much like the medicine ball squat press except that with this movement you perform a two-hand underhand throw as high as possible.

Complex Exercises

The complex exercises included in the training program require speed and explosiveness; plus, the front squat puts absolute strength in the area of the hips and upper legs. Going from an explosive movement such as a hang clean, to a basic strength movement such as a front squat, to another explosive exercise such as a push press is a great way to stimulate the muscular nervous system and speed up your metabolic rate (i.e., burn calories).

Hang Clean to Front Squat to Push Press

Go from one lift to the other, making a smooth transition between exercises. Perform one rep and then go on to the next exercise in the movement. As you finish the clean, keep your elbows up and, with the bar supported on your shoulders, go right into a front squat. As you finish the squat, rebend at the knees and explode up into a push press.

Romanian Deadlift to Dumbbell Press

Romanian deadlifts (RDLs) are great for working the hamstrings and lower back. Start by holding a pair of dumbbells in front of your thighs while standing erect. As you take the dumbbells down in front of your legs, your hips should go back. As you go down, also keep your lower back arched and your abdominals tight. Bring the dumbbells down until you feel a good and comfortable stretch in your hamstrings. As you come up, your lower back muscles take over to bring your upper body to an erect position. After completing the movement, go directly into a dumbbell press, keeping the dumbbells close to your body. When the dumbbells reach your upper chest area, bring your elbows under your shoulders and face your palms forward. When you have fully achieved this position, extend the dumbbells upward. Bring the dumbbells down to the starting position and repeat the movement.

Dumbbell Hammer Curl to Dumbbell Push Press

Start by performing a hammer curl. While bringing the dumbbells up into a curl position with your thumbs up (dumbbells at or near the top of your shoulders), bend at the knees, bring your hips back, and go directly into a squat position. When you have achieved this position, go directly into your push press. When your arms are fully extended, bring the dumbbells down by your side and repeat the movement.

Matrix Workouts

Each matrix workout takes you through three planes of movement: the frontal plane, which goes from side to side; the sagittal plane, which goes forward and backward; and the transverse plane, which covers rotational movements. Most matrix workouts use dumbbells for work in the transverse plane, but I prefer to use a medicine ball because it is more specific to the game of basketball.

Matrix I

With the dumbbells or a medicine ball down by your side and facing forward, perform a front lunge with the dumbbells coming out to your forward ankle. After doing this with each leg, perform a side lunge facing forward and to the right, bringing the dumbbells (or medicine ball) again to the ankle of your outermost leg. Now go back to the starting position. Using your right leg, open your hips up and back to a 45-degree angle and lunge again with only your right leg, bringing the dumbbells (or medicine ball) down to your ankles. Go back to the starting position, lunge forward with the other leg, and perform the same combination. Make sure that when you take the dumbbells or medicine ball down to your ankles you keep your chest up and shoulders back as much as possible. Tall men and women may want to take the dumbbells or medicine ball down to just below the knee to lessen the strain on the lower back.

Matrix II

This exercise is the same as the matrix I, except that after each lunge you perform a pressing movement. Make a smooth transition between the lunge and the pressing movement.

Plyometrics and Jumping Drills

The question I am asked the most by both coaches and athletes is, What exercises can I do to help me jump higher? The answer is a combination of both resistance exercises and certain types of explosive jumping drills called plyometrics. Plyometrics are drills that link strength with speed of movement to produce power. Plyometric training is essential to athletes who jump, lift, or run.

The major purpose of such exercises is to heighten the excitability of the nervous system for improved reactive ability of the neuromuscular system. The physical basis for plyometric training is found in the rebound movement patterns so prevalent in basketball skills. This is why plyometrics and jump training can be so vital to your overall improvement as a basketball player.

Most of the plyometric programs that I have used over the years have had too many jumping drills for the athlete to perform. One must understand that the game of basketball is made up largely of vertical jumping skills that include rebounding, defending, and shooting. Because of this, a player must take care of the joints of the ankles, knees, and hips. Too much jumping can be just as bad as not enough jumping. This is why I have incorporated plyometric and jumping drills into the resistance program. By following the off-season resistance work, you will obtain the strength base needed before starting the plyometric and jumping drills in the preseason training program.

Jumping Program Guidelines

1. Do not perform jumping drills two consecutive days. The workouts in this program have you performing plyometrics no more than twice a week and on alternate days.
2. Remember that speed may be more important than resistance.
3. Remember that specificity of movement, which your workout includes, is necessary for carryover to athletic activities.
4. Use good footwear and a padded or soft surface for jumping.
5. Perform each plyometric exercise to maximum effort to stimulate the neuromuscular system.
6. Build a good strength base before starting extensive plyometric training. The 52-week program provides this solid base.
7. When jumping or landing, always keep the knee in line with the second or third toe. Do not rotate internally. This is especially important for female players.

Nine plyometric and jumping exercises are included as part of the resistance training program. This leaves no guesswork as to what drills you should do during a workout.

Dumbbell Jump

While holding a dumbbell in each hand and with your feet shoulder-width apart, go down into a quarter squat position; then explode up as fast as possible. When landing, you may stop, reset, and jump again or go right down into a quarter squat position and jump again.

Medicine Ball Jump

Using a medicine ball that weighs between 8 and 15 pounds, secure it with both hands at upper chest level. Begin the movement by squatting until the hamstrings are parallel to the floor. Remember to keep the hips back and the chest up. Do not bend over at the hips. As soon as you hit the bottom position, jump and explode upward as high as possible. At the same time extend your arms and the ball upward as high as you can. As soon as you hit the floor, bend the knees, force the hips back (to dissipate the force of the landing), and repeat the jump and movement.

Repetitive Quick Jump

This movement is the same as the medicine ball jump without a medicine ball. The height of the jump is also different because you descend only a quarter of the way into a full squat before you immediately jump back up and repeat the movement.

Dumbbell Squat Thrust and Jump

While holding a dumbbell in each hand, perform a squat thrust; then, when coming up, explode and jump as high as possible. When landing, bend your knees, go down into another squat thrust position, and repeat the movement.

MVP Shuttle

With your legs bent at 90 degrees, jump out as far as possible while extending your legs fully. When landing, bend your knees and repeat the movement as fast as possible. When hitting the platform, keep your feet shoulder-width apart and your lower back flat. You may also perform the shuttle with single-leg movements and jumps. Make sure you land on your toes with a soft touch when coming back to the platform. This applies to both single- and double-leg jumps.

Be creative with different types of jumping and foot quickness drills. The sky is the limit! One foot quickness drill on the shuttle that I like is the five-point dot drill. Place five dots on the platform (athletic tape works well), one in the middle and the other four in each corner of the platform. Using a single leg, go from one dot to the other, forming an hourglass shape. Go around three times with one leg, and then three times with the other. You must be quick with your feet yet explosive and in control of your foot and your entire leg. Keep your knees in line with your second and third toes.

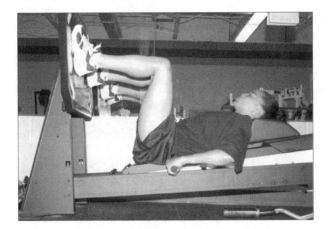
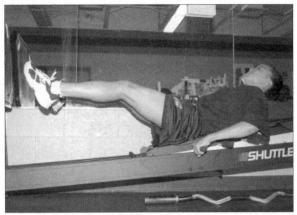

Dumbbell Split Jump

With one foot forward and the other back (each 8 to 10 inches from midline) and holding a dumbbell in each hand, jump up as high as possible, switching places with each foot. As soon as you hit the ground, bend your knees and jump again, switching foot placement each time. Keep your toes pointed straight ahead and your knees flexed when landing.

Box Jump-Up

Box jumps-ups are a great way to increase vertical jump. Stand facing the box with your feet shoulder-width apart and your toes pointed straight. Explode up on the box. As soon as you land, hop back down and repeat the jump. It is important to explode up as soon as your feet hit the floor. Avoid too much upper body lean when jumping; keep your chest up and out. Bend at the knees and not at the waist. Make sure the box will not move when you land on top. Box height will vary, but a general rule is to start with a box height equal to your vertical jump. If your vertical jump is 28 inches, then start with a box that is around 28 inches high and add box height as you get stronger.

Single-Leg Vertical Jump

This exercise is similar to the box jump-up except that you are jumping off one leg. When jumping down, land on both legs to protect the knee joints. Be sure to bend your knees to dissipate the force. After landing with both feet, immediately explode back up on one leg. Box height will be a quarter to a half of what you use for both legs; you can build it up as your legs get stronger.

Lateral Box Jump

Lateral box jumps are a great way to improve lateral movement and are often used with footwork drills. Start with 15 seconds and work up to 30-second work intervals. If you go 15 seconds, your goal is 15 or more contacts on the box. If you go 30 seconds, your goal is 30 contacts or more on the box. On this particular drill you are jumping up on the box, then down on the other side. Immediately jump back up and then down the other side. Both feet should hit the surface at the same time.

Tubing and Running Resistance Exercises

The following exercises use surgical tubing as a form of resistance. You can find this type of tubing in most fitness or sport catalogs. Some of the running exercises listed in this section use something as simple as a wall for resistance. Using resistance when doing these movements improves not only muscular endurance but also explosiveness and acceleration. Be sure that when you finish any of these drills and movements you perform the same movement without the resistance tubing so you can achieve a contrast training effect. When you've finished doing the drills against a wall, go directly to sprinting down the gym floor. You'll really feel the difference!

Sidewinder

This drill is a great way to increase lateral speed and quickness. Place the resistance bands on your ankles as shown. These are the five basic movements:

1. Perform a basic W down the court and back. Really power out with the lead leg. Make sure your feet do not cross over. Stay low and keep your abdominals tight and your chest up and out.

2. Do a basic power step walk laterally. Some people call this a "monster walk," with the lead leg and hip coming up and out as far as possible, then the leg that follows sliding back to the starting position.

3. Do a regular high-knee pump from baseline to baseline. Keep your knees in line with your feet. Keep your feet from flaring out when running.

4. A great exercise to combine with the sidewinder is the power skip. Perform a regular skip, but drive the forward knee as high as possible.

5. Perform a regular walking lunge. When walking with the bands on your ankles, really power out with a big step, trying to bring your feet up and out as far as possible. Be sure to keep your upper body from leaning over. Your knee should be over your toes when stepping out. The back knee should almost hit the floor when walking.

Viper Jump

Our players like this vertical jumping drill using resistance bands. When jumping, bend and flex at the knees, not at the waist. Keep your body upright with your chest up and out as you jump. When you jump, reach as high as possible with your arms fully extended. When landing, stabilize your body by keeping your feet shoulder-width apart and your knees bent. As soon as you land, flex your knees immediately and jump again.

Another drill that I use with the belt (viper) is a stationary power skip. One player has the belt around the waist while performing a stationary power skip. A partner holds the bands down with the hands or feet. After 10 skips, the partner releases the band and the player sprints 30 yards down the court. The contrast training effect will really help that all-important explosiveness and acceleration.

Harness Run

When harness running or performing resistance sprints such as pulling a sled, maintaining good running form is very important. Be sure you have a good forward body lean, and keep your head and eyes looking straight ahead. Bring your knees

high when running, with your forward and up knee in line with your foot. Do not flare your knee out or pull it in. Keep your elbows in and your hands relaxed. Work your arms as though you were beating a drum, moving your hands from your jaw to your hip joint.

Wall Run

With your arms straight out against a wall, drive your knees up as high as possible with good forward body lean. When doing this drill, drive your knees up as fast as possible, staying on your toes for faster leg action.

Wall Quick Feet

This exercise is a resistance running drill as well as a foot quickness drill. Start by having one knee flexed up and one leg extended with the foot on the floor. Stay on your toes throughout the movement, and maintain at least a 45-degree lean into the wall during the entire drill. When starting, push against the wall and at the same time drive your knees until you have three foot contacts on the floor; then stop immediately with the knee up. Pause and start again, driving your legs as fast as possible. The count should be 1-2-3, 1-2-3, 1-2-3. When starting with the right knee up, you will finish with the left knee up.

CHAPTER 8

Basketball-Specific Conditioning Drills

Chapter 1 addresses the importance of specific conditioning for basketball. One concept related to this that I have saved for this chapter is the SAID

principle—*s*pecific *a*daptations to *i*mposed *d*emands. As you know, basketball is a game of short, powerful stop-and-go sprints, explosive jumps, lateral sliding, and rotational movements. To be able to perform these movements day after day and practice after practice, the body conditions itself cardiovascularly and muscularly. The result is a lean and muscular athlete.

You may ask yourself, then, why you need to add conditioning if basketball itself conditions athletes. The answer is that it takes a properly designed conditioning program to produce the right kind of stress and intensity so that your body can condition itself specifically for practice and, more important, game situations. The results, which you will see from doing these particular workouts, will help you become a better basketball player.

During a basketball game your ability to perform must be the same in the fourth quarter as it is in the

So that she can start and finish strong each and every game, Andrea Stinson works hard on her conditioning.

Photo courtesy of the Charlotte Sting

179

first or second quarter. Your ability to hit a jump shot after sprinting down the court full speed determines your success and the success of your team. Your off-season, preseason, and in-season workouts and conditioning have been carefully planned to fit your all-around needs in the development of your all-around game.

This chapter details the drills listed in your day-by-day workouts in chapters 2 through 5. Some drills are strictly running conditioning drills and others include shooting a basketball. Other coaches and I have used many different conditioning and shooting drills over the years. I encourage you to include others that you like and are familiar with. The ones detailed in this chapter have brought great results to NBA, WNBA, and college players.

Wall Run

The wall run (see chapter 7, page 180) is not only a good power-building exercise but also an important part of basketball-specific conditioning. This is a great tool to use either with your resistance running or your regular conditioning work. Perform the drill in either 15- or 30-second intervals with a 1:3 work-to-rest ratio (e.g., if you work 15 seconds, then rest 45 seconds). As you get closer to the start of the regular season, go to a 1:2 work-to-rest ratio.

300-Yard Shuttle

The 300-yard shuttle distance is based on a regulation basketball court and can be used as a test (as noted in chapter 1) as well as a drill. To begin the test, start behind the baseline and sprint to the opposite free throw line (which is 25 yards). Touch it with your foot; then sprint back to the baseline. A total of 12 touches or 6 trips up and back completes 300 yards (25 × 12 = 300). Rest five minutes; then repeat the drill. Average the two times together to get your running time and compare your time to the testing times found on page 15 in chapter 1.

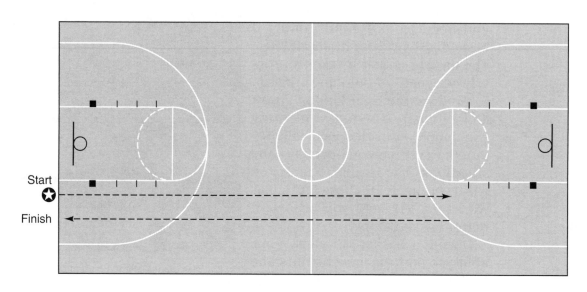

17 Drill

Start on the sideline and sprint to the opposite sideline. Repeat for a total of 17 sprints. Across and back equals two sprints, so you will finish on the opposite side from where you started. After you rest for 2:30 to 2:45, perform another set of 17 sprints. Average the times together to get your running time and compare to the following table.

Position	Time to beat (in seconds)	
	Pro or college players	High school players
Point guard	61	64
Shooting guard and small forward	63	66
Power forward	65	68
Center	67	70

4, 8, 16 Drill

This drill involves running across the court from sideline to sideline. Start on one sideline and sprint to the other side and back for a total of four sprints (across and back equals two sprints). You should complete this in 15 seconds or less. Rest 30 seconds; then get ready for the second sprint—four times down and back (a total of eight sprints). You should complete this in 30 seconds or less. Rest 60 seconds; then get ready for the third set—eight times down and back for a total of 16 sprints. Complete this last set in 60 seconds or less.

Ladder Sprint

Start on the baseline and sprint to the opposite baseline in 5 seconds. Rest for 10 seconds. Then sprint the length of the court three times in 15 seconds or less. Rest 30 seconds. Then, sprint the length of the court five times in 30 seconds or less. Rest 60 seconds. Finally, sprint the length of the court seven times in 45 seconds or less. Do not run the last ladder of seven sprints until you can run the first three groups of ladders in the required times.

Gassers

This drill involves acceleration, deceleration, and change of direction. Start on one baseline, sprint to the nearest free throw line and back, sprint to the half court and back, sprint to the far free throw line and back, and finally to the far baseline and back (see diagram on next page). At the end of each sprint your foot must touch the line before you turn and sprint to the next line. Running time should be 32 seconds or less with 90 seconds of recovery time between repetitions.

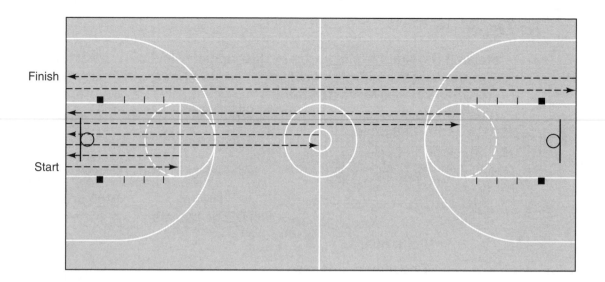

30-Second Gassers

Starting on the baseline, sprint to the opposite baseline, touch the line with your foot, and then turn and sprint back to the starting baseline. Your goal is to cross the entire length of the court as many times as possible in 30 seconds. If you do not make it the entire length of the court, mark where you finish and try to beat that mark in the next set or workout. Take 90 seconds to recover between repetitions.

Four Corner Drill

The goal of this drill is to perform it in the shortest amount of time possible. Start in one corner of the court and sprint to the opposite baseline; then power slide shuffle along that baseline to the corner, backpedal to the starting baseline, and finish by power slide shuffling across the starting baseline. Do not cross your feet when doing your power slide shuffles. Be sure you are facing down court during the entire drill. Recover for 90 seconds between repetitions.

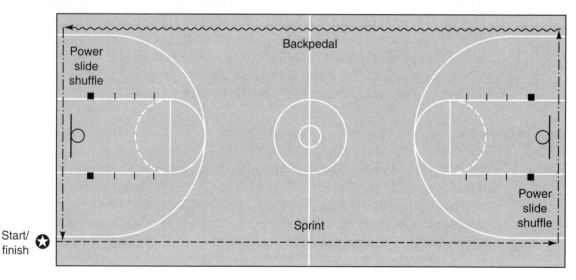

Opposite Hand Layup

The goal of this drill is to cross the lane diagonally from one corner of the free throw line as many times as possible in 60 seconds. Starting from beyond one corner of the free throw line, dribble diagonally across the lane and perform layups with your non-dominant hand. Dribble back to the starting position with your dominant hand. Recover for 90 seconds between repetitions.

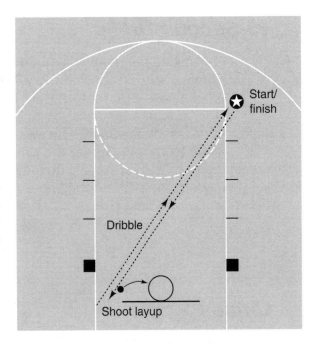

Rim Touch

Stand directly under the front of the goal. Jump as high as possible for the prescribed number of jumps (noted in your particular workout). Keep your knees in line with your second or third toes when jumping and landing. Do not rotate internally. This is especially important for female players. Reach as high as possible on each jump with your arms on each side of the net or rim. When you have completed your jumps, pick up the basketball and dribble down to the other basket for a jump shot or layup. When you have made the shot, repeat the number of jumps, and then continue the drill for a total of 50 to 100 jumps. Start out by doing 5 jumps at each basket and work up to 10 as your conditioning improves.

Crosscourt Sprint and Shoot

Start by shooting a jump shot at the top of the key; then sprint to either side of the court (1) and back to the top of the key or the elbow (2) to receive a pass and do a jump shot. After your jump shot, sprint to the closest sideline (3), then sprint to the opposite sideline (4) and back to the key or elbow (5) to shoot again. Continue the pattern, adding an extra sideline run before the jump shot each time through until you are crossing the court a total of five times. Finish the drill by shooting 5 to 10 free throws. Repeat the sequence two or three times.

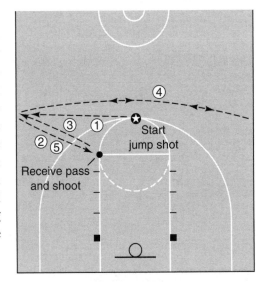

55-Second Drill

Starting on the right wing (spot 1), shoot as many shots as possible in 55 seconds off of a pass. You must move 7 to 10 feet side to side after each shot. At 55 seconds, shoot 5 to 10 free throws and then move to spot 2. Repeat the process and then move to spot 3. Add up the shots you made from each of the three positions and total your score.

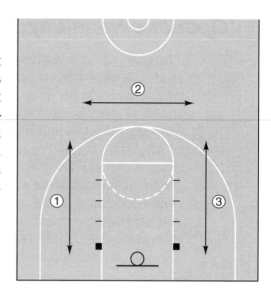

Circle Pass

Have a partner or coach pass you a ball as you run around five yards outside the midcourt circle. Catch the ball with one hand and pass it back with the same hand while running in the circle. After five catches, reverse the direction of the run.

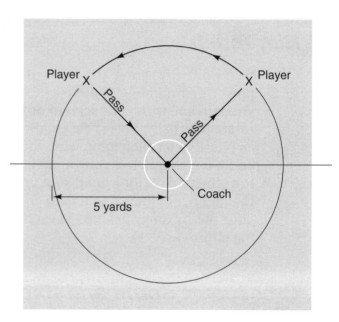

Shooting W

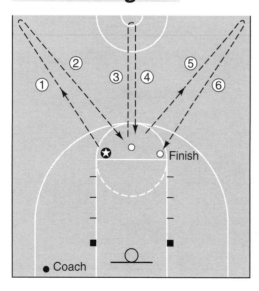

Shoot a jump shot at either elbow of the lane; then sprint to either half-court corner (1). Sprint back to the free throw circle or top of the key for another jump shot (2). Then sprint to the midcourt circle (3) and back to the key (4) and repeat another jump shot in the free throw circle. After the second shot, sprint to the opposite half-court corner (5) and back (6) for a third jump shot at the free throw circle or top of the key. If you miss the shot, grab the rebound for a "put-back." If you make the shot, the coach will rebound the ball. Three shots constitute one set. Work up to three to five shots. Shoot three to five free throws; then repeat.

Rebounder Cross the Lane, Shoot, and Sprint

Have a rebounder available at the basket. Start by shooting 10 shots (miss or make) while you run back and forth from point A on one side of the lane to the same point on the other side. After you finish your last shot, immediately sprint to the opposite baseline and back. After your sprint, shoot (miss or make) five free throws. After your free throws, repeat the process at point B, but this time, after your 10 shots, sprint down to the opposite baseline and back twice, and then shoot your five free throws. After your free throws, repeat the process at point C, but this time, after your 10 shots, sprint to the opposite baseline and back three

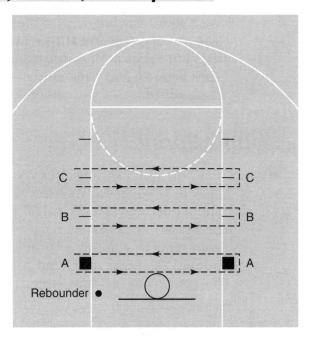

times, and then shoot your five free throws. Be sure to keep a record of your shooting makes and misses, including your free throws. You must be able to hit free throws when you are tired.

Backboard Slap and Sprint

Start at point A. Jump up and slap the backboard three times; then sprint to point B and pull up for a jump shot. After the jump shot, backpedal on your toes to point C and slap the backboard three times; then sprint to point D at the free throw circle and pull up for another jump shot. Backpedal on your toes to point E and slap the backboard three times and sprint to point F for another jump shot. Make five free throws and repeat.

If you cannot hit the backboard with your hand, hang a piece of rope from the backboard. As your vertical jump improves, you can decrease the length of the rope until you are hitting the backboard.

Keep your knees in line with

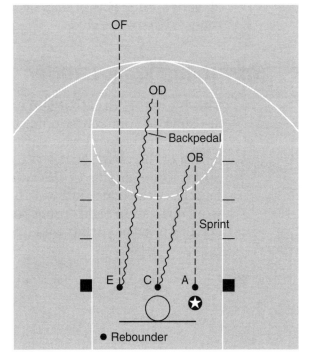

your second or third toes when jumping and landing. Do not rotate internally. This is especially important for female players.

Team Free Throw and Sprint

With your team lined up on the baseline, have one player on the free throw line. The player on the free throw line shoots two free throws. If the first shot misses, the entire team sprints down and back twice. If the second shot misses, the team sprints down and back only once. If the player makes the free throw, the team does not run. Every member of the team takes turns shooting free throws.

Uphill Sprint

Perform uphill sprints after your track work. The degree or grade of the hill can vary depending on what is available near your track. The distance up the hill should be between 40 and 60 yards. Be sure to drive your knees up high and drive your arms up and back as hard as possible when sprinting. When driving your arms as you run, your hands should go from jaw to hip with an open and relaxed fist. Keep your head still and your face relaxed. Walk back down the hill for your recovery time, which should be 60 to 90 seconds.

Metabolic Sprint

Use this drill in place of one of the required drills on one of your conditioning days when you are doing some short sprint work. Perform the drill on a track or football field. Start by sprinting 20 yards, resting 10 seconds, then sprinting 30 yards, resting 10 seconds. Continue lengthening the sprint to 40, 50, and then 60 yards with 10 seconds of rest after each one. Once you have reached the 60-yard sprint, repeat it and come back down the ladder to a 50-, 40-, 30-, and 20-yard sprint. This equals one set. Work up to three sets with two minutes of recovery between sets.

Sprint and Walk Ladder

This is another drill that you can use in place of one of the required drills that are done on your conditioning days. Perform this drill as a team or individually. Start on the baseline and sprint to the opposite baseline; then walk back one length of the court. Sprint two lengths of the court and walk back one length. Sprint three lengths of the court and walk back one length. Then sprint four lengths of the court and walk back one length. As your conditioning improves, work up to six to eight "rungs" of the ladder. You may also work down the ladder, starting at eight sprints and descending to one.

Agility, Balance, and Ball-Handling Drills

Agility, footwork, balance, and ball-handling skills are all important aspects of today's game of basketball; they are also skills that all players must master to reach their maximum potential. Some athletes are born with the ability to change direction or move their feet quickly. Some may be able control their balance and stability even during contact. Some players can even make a basketball do what they want it to do the very first time they dribble one. However, most people have to work each day on an area of their game to see improvement.

You *can* improve your agility. You *can* learn to move your feet more quickly. You *can* also create more stability in your game and learn to dribble a basketball at a higher skill level if you just take the time to work and dedicate yourself to getting better each day, at every practice and at game time. The exercises in this chapter give you specific ways to improve these skills.

Agility and Footwork

Agility is the ability to change direction quickly and explosively while maintaining balance and control. In training in which you move forward, backward, or laterally, your objective is to generate maximum muscular force to accelerate the body in any given direction as quickly and as forcefully as possible. Power gives you acceleration, and with acceleration also comes velocity (which is speed in any direction).

Basketball involves not only forward, backward, and lateral movements that require agility but also complex movements such as running down the court and jumping vertically for a shot without hesitation. Another example of a complex movement is side-shuffling to guard your man during defensive play and then instantly sprinting down the court because you or someone else has stolen the ball.

Having good foot quickness goes hand in hand with your agility work. Everyone wants solid, balanced, and controlled footwork and foot quickness. Often a power forward or center makes a spin move at the lower post position and is called for traveling, or a guard tries to beat his man off the dribble and loses control of the ball and is called for too many steps. You must work on certain moves that you are going to execute in a game situation, but you must also spend time working on footwork and agility to help perform those moves at a higher level of skill and quickness. To have good footwork and good foot speed, you must train at that speed, but it must be in a fast but controlled manner.

Working on your agility with the drills provided in this section will improve your ability to change direction quickly, easily, and forcefully. Perhaps a less common term for agility is *dynamic balance*. Both terms refer to the ability to control

Footwork is one of the keys to success for Baron Davis.

shifts in the body's center of gravity, whether those shifts are horizontal, vertical, circular, linear, or multidirectional.

When performing the drills that are in your workout program, start with slow, controlled actions to give your feet, legs, and the rest of your body some positive feedback on the movements and patterns you are trying to execute. As you get comfortable with the drills, start moving faster and faster. However, speed is not of any value unless it is under control. Any race car driver will tell you the same thing. Always have good technique, balance, and control when doing the agility drills or when you are out on the court playing and practicing.

The agility and footwork drills that are scheduled into each week of your year-round training program are detailed here. Do not hesitate, after your scheduled drill, to add one or two of the other drills listed in this section, if time allows.

In addition to the drills in this section, you can also use the plyometric drill and resistance tubing drills in chapter 7 (pages 172 to 178) to improve agility and footwork, particularly the lateral box jump and wall quick feet drills.

Jump Rope Routine

This jump rope routine is based on a square with four quadrants numbered as shown. Perform each of the following drills in the order shown. If you struggle to finish all 10 drills in one session, work up week by week until you can successfully complete all of them.

1. Regular jumping × 50
2. Jumping side to side with both feet, 4 to 3 and back × 50
3. Up and back, 4 to 1 and back × 50
4. Boxer shuffle, 2 on right foot, 2 on left foot × 50
5. Up and back on one foot, 4 to 1 and back × 25 each foot
6. Side to side on one foot, 4 to 3 × 25 each foot
7. Triangle (1, 2, 4) alternate and switch (2, 1, 3) × 25
8. Four square jumping using both feet, then switch to just one, 1, 2, 3, 4 × 10 rounds
9. Double jump with bounce, rope under foot twice × 50
10. Bonus jump. Do as many regular jumps as you can in 30 seconds (110 times is the number to beat).

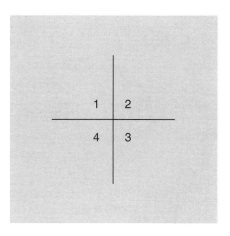

Home Base

Stand in the middle of the lane in a defensive position. Note the numbered positions on the figure of the court. You can put blocks on the court with these numbers. On a coach's command, run in place. The coach then calls out a number for you to move to. Move to that numbered position as fast as possible and then return to home base, at which point the coach calls out another number. When the coach calls out numbers 2 or 3, sprint to those positions; then power slide shuffle back to home base. When the coach calls out positions 1 or 4, power slide shuffle there and back. The drill should last 25 to 30 seconds, and you should touch with your foot as many numbered blocks as possible.

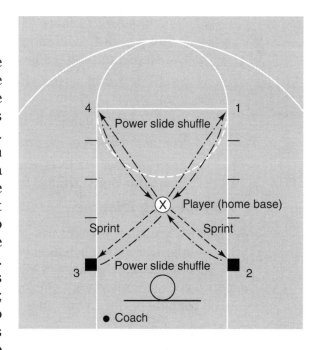

Dot Drills

Some of the best foot quickness drills begin with dot drills and line drills. No equipment is needed except some athletic tape to make dots (see figure).

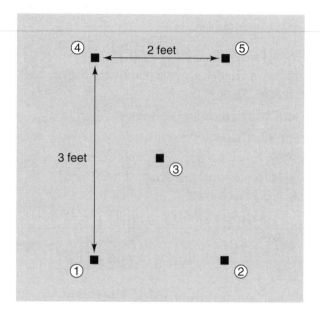

Five Parts

This drill consists of five segments, each of which is done down and back three times. The goal is to complete all five segments in 30 seconds or less.

1. *Down and back.* Start with feet split, one foot on dot 1 and one on dot 2. Jump to dot 3 with both feet, then to dots 4 and 5 with feet split. Repeat the steps jumping backward.
2. *Single-leg hop* using the right foot. Form a figure eight down and back.
3. *Single-leg hop* using the left foot. Form a figure eight.
4. *Hop with both feet together.* Form a figure eight.
5. *Turn around.* This is the same as "down and back," except that you turn your body around to go in the other direction.

Single-Leg Triangle

Hop on your left leg to form a triangle in a counterclockwise direction for 10 seconds; then switch legs and perform the same movement for 10 seconds (2-3-1-2). Go back to the left leg and form a triangle in a clockwise direction for 10 seconds. Repeat with the right leg (1-3-2-1). Count how many times around the triangle pattern you can go in 10 seconds with each leg.

Single-Leg Z

Form a Z pattern (4-5-3-1-2) using one leg. See how fast you can get from the top of the Z to the bottom with each leg. You may also form a Z with both feet together.

Single-Leg M

Form an M pattern (4-5-3-2-1) using one leg. See how fast you can form the pattern with each leg. Again, you may use both feet, keeping them close together, side by side.

Line Drills

Find a straight line anywhere on the floor from one to two feet in length (or make one using athletic tape). When performing line drills, make sure your feet are moving as fast as possible, yet keep them under control. Stay light on your feet with little sound coming from the contacts on the ground. Each drill should last anywhere from 10 to 15 seconds.

1. **Front jump.** Face the line and jump over and back with feet together.
2. **Side jump.** Jump over the line sideways with feet together.
3. **Side step 1-2.** With the line beside you, step over with one foot, then the other, and step back over the same way.
4. **Front step 1-2.** With the line in front of you, step over with one foot, then the other, and back over the same way.
5. **Side hop.** With the line beside you, hop over with one leg, then the other. The trail leg comes over the line but does not touch the ground. As soon as the trail leg goes over the line, hop back across to the other side of the line and repeat the side hops, being as light on your feet as possible.
6. **Single-leg hop.** Jump over the line sideways and back on a single leg.
7. **Switch hop.** Start with the line in front of you, with your right foot on one side and your left foot on the other. Jump and switch foot positions as quickly as possible, moving your feet backward and forward.
8. **Side switch hop.** Start with your feet straddling the line. Hop quickly with your right foot going over to the other side of the line at the same time as your left foot goes over to where your right foot was. Start with your right foot moving in front of your left. After 15 seconds do the same drill with your left foot moving over your right.

Lane Agility Box

Set up four cones, one on each corner of the free throw lane as shown in the diagram. If using a high-school court in which the lane is 12 feet across, move each cone out 2 feet so that they form a lane 16 feet across (this is the size on which the times below are based). Start beside one cone in a two-point stance. Sprint to the baseline cone; then power slide shuffle facing away from the court to and past the second baseline cone. When past the second baseline cone, backpedal to and past the elbow cone, then power slide shuffle across and past the starting cone. When you pass the starting cone, reverse the process by power slide shuffling across the free throw line, sprinting to the baseline cone, and power slide shuffling across the baseline. When you are past the baseline cone, backpedal to and past the start/finish cone and compare your time to the table. Perform three to four sets with 45 seconds rest between each.

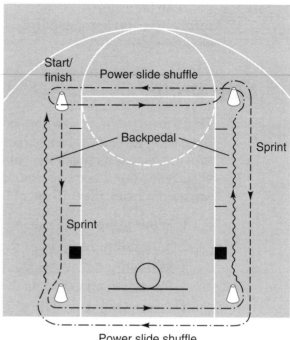

Position	Time for males (s)	Time for females (s)
Guards	10.2 to 10.9	13.0 to 14.5
Forwards	11.0 to 11.4	14.6 to 15.5
Centers	11.5 to 12.3	14.6 to 15.5

Quick Feet Box Step

Find a stable box that is 12 to 15 inches high. Start with one foot on the box and one foot on the floor, with your toes pointed straight ahead and your upper body in an erect neutral position. On command, move the foot that is on the box to the floor and the foot on the floor to the box. Keep switching foot positions for 15 to 30 seconds. Move as quickly as possible with your feet while still staying under control (meaning that no extra upper body motion occurs except arm and shoulder movement as if you were running).

Lane Slide

Start directly at the bottom of the free throw circle facing the baseline. On command, power slide shuffle in either direction, touching the line with your foot; then shuffle across the lane to the opposite line. Continue shuffling back and forth for 30 seconds. See how many times you can cross and touch each line without crossing your feet. Your goal should be 25 or more line touches in 30 seconds.

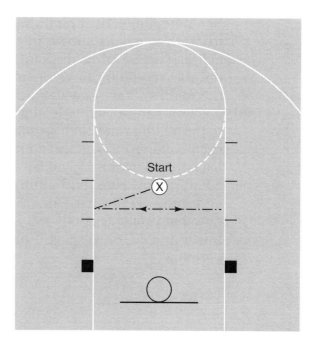

Half-Court Layup Agility Drill

Start at the midcourt corner. Run in and receive a pass at the three-point line; then come in for a jump shot at the elbow or a layup. After the shot or layup, power slide shuffle across to the other side of the court facing the baseline. When you are at the corner of the baseline/sideline, backpedal on your toes to the hash mark. Turn quickly and sprint to the midcourt corner; then turn and run to the nearest elbow while receiving a pass at the three-point line. Repeat the drill to the other side of the court. Performing this drill to one side of the court and then the other counts as one repetition. Work up to two to three sets of five reps while shooting 10 free throws between sets.

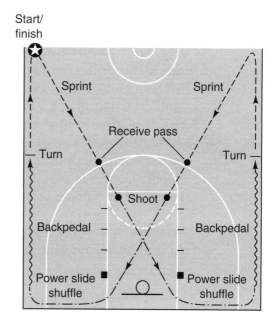

Star Agility Drill

Use nine cones or athletic tape to make a star as shown in the figure. The tip of each point of the star should be 15 yards from the middle. Start in a defensive position and power slide shuffle to the middle cone; then sprint to each cone or marker and shuffle back to the middle. Try different combination runs and shuffles and even backward runs. See how many outside cones you can touch in a 30- to 45-second time period.

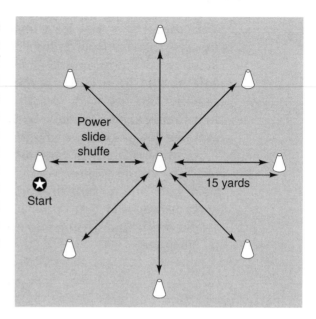

Triangle Slide

Set up three cones (or use athletic tape) to form a triangle that is equal on all sides. Place one cone or tape marking three feet beyond the free throw line. Place the other cones or tape two to three feet to the outside of the lane. Starting at the cone above the free throw line and facing midcourt, power slide shuffle to either of the midpost markers or cones. Continue across the lane to the other marker or cone, then back to the top marker or cone. See how many cones you can get to in a 30-second time period.

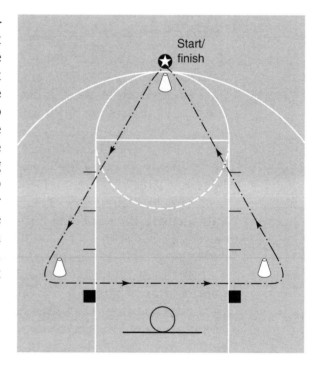

T *Slide*

Set up four cones 10 yards apart in a T formation. Start by sprinting to the middle of the T; then slide shuffle to the cone on the right, turn, and sprint to the one on the far left. Continue by slide shuffling to the middle of the T (while facing the start/finish cone); then sprint past the start/finish cone. Be creative by trying different combinations of runs and shuffles.

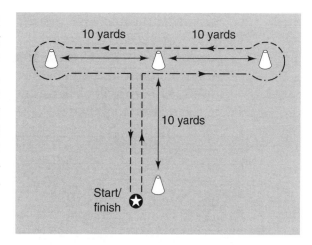

Reverse 7 Drill

Set up three cones or pieces of tape 12 to 15 yards apart to make the shape of a 7 (see diagram). This is very similar to the triangle drill, except that in this drill you are only doing two-thirds of the triangle. Start by sprinting to cone 2, then backpedaling to cone 3. As soon as you pass the third cone, accelerate and sprint back to cone 2. When passing cone 2, assume a low position and power slide shuffle to the start/finish cone. Once again, try different combinations of sprints and shuffles; you can even add two to five vertical jumps when you reach each cone.

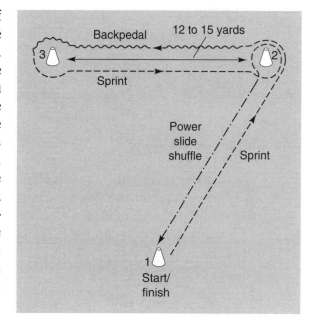

Pattern Run I

Starting at the baseline, sprint to the top of the key at the other end of the court, where you receive a pass from your partner or coach. At the elbow, shoot a jumper or go in for a layup. After your shot, do five quick backboard taps, backpedal on your toes to half court, and perform five deep power jumps. After your jumps, slide shuffle back to the baseline. Goal time to complete the drill should be three sets, each under 45 seconds. Shoot 10 free throws between sets.

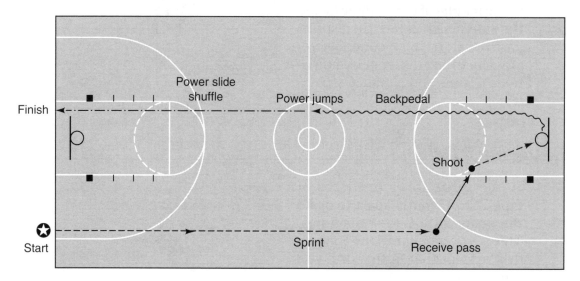

Pattern Run II

Pattern runs may also be performed using commands from a coach or partner. Your coach starts you by shouting "sprint," and at any time may again shout or point to the direction of your slide shuffle or backward run or have you sprint forward again to finish the drill. The drill should last between 30 and 45 seconds.

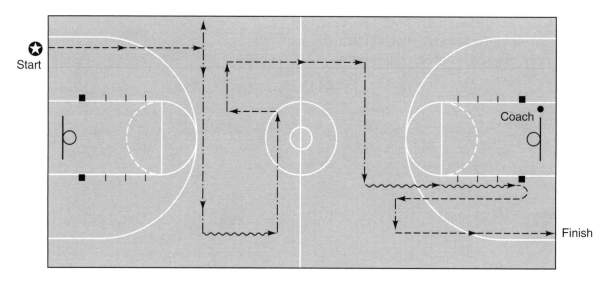

Tennis Ball Drop

Stand 7 to 10 feet from a coach or partner, who drops a tennis ball from shoulder height. When the ball is dropped, sprint to catch it before it bounces a second time. After each catch, keep moving back farther and farther from the coach or partner. See how far you can be from your coach and still catch the ball before the second bounce. Alternatively you can stand with your back to the coach and, on the coach's command, turn around as quickly as possible and sprint to catch the ball. The coach or partner can also hold out two tennis balls (one on each side) and drop only one ball.

Cone or Minihurdle Jumps

You can perform many different types of jumps and hops over cones or minihurdles. Focus on staying on your toes and jumping as fast as possible while remaining under control and maintaining your balance. Cones or minihurdles should be 6½ to 12 inches in height. Each repetition should last 10 to 15 seconds.

1. **Double-Leg Jump.** Face the cone and jump over each hurdle, landing on both feet. As soon as you land, turn to face the cone and double-leg jump again.

2. **Double-Leg Side Jump.** Stand to the side of the cone and perform double-leg jumps, taking off and landing on both feet. Jump back as fast as possible.

3. **Single-Leg Side Jump.** Perform the side jump drill, but take off and land on one foot. Switch feet and repeat. This drill is great for balance because when you land with only one foot, you must regain your balance and control before jumping back over the hurdle.

4. **Split Jump.** Start by straddling the cone or hurdle. Jump straight up as high as possible, bringing your feet together (side by side) in midair and back down to straddle the hurdle. You can also perform this drill by facing the minihurdle and putting your right foot on one side of the hurdle and your left foot on the other side. Jump up as high as possible while switching your foot position in mid-air. You'll come down with your right foot back on one side and your left foot in front on the other side. As soon as you hit the ground on your toes, spring back up and repeat the movement. Stay light on your toes and move your legs quickly but with control throughout the drill.

5. **Single-Leg Half Jump**. Standing beside the cone or minihurdle with your left leg nearest the hurdle, jump over the hurdle starting from your right leg. When your left foot hits the ground on the other side, your right leg follows but only until it is directly over the top of the cone or hurdle. At this point, push with your left leg to go back over. When your right leg hits the ground on the other side, your left leg goes directly over the top of the hurdle. Repeat the process as fast as possible, staying on your toes and light on your feet as you jump from side to side.

6. **Crossover Step.** While standing beside the cone, take your outside leg and cross it over your inside leg and the hurdle or cone. Upon landing

on the opposite side of the cone, perform a 1-2-3 step sequence before initiating the crossover to the other side. Getting your rhythm is an important factor in performing this and many other footwork drills. Keep your shoulders square and your chest up, and land softly on your toes. You can also perform this movement by taking the outside foot behind your body while stepping over the minihurdle. Again it is important that you have good rhythm with your feet (1-2-3 step when landing on the opposite side of the hurdle). Make sure you turn your hips and bring your knees high while stepping over the hurdle. This helps make the transition to the other side of the hurdle easier and more fluid.

Balance

Being able to keep your balance and stabilize yourself while under the basket fighting for a rebound or backing your defender down while trying to get where you should be on the court is another important factor in the overall success of your game.

Balance or stability training works the deep "slow-twitch" muscle fibers of the ankles, knees, and especially the hips. Regardless of whether you have a natural sense of balance or are balance-challenged, these drills will help you improve your game. Three systems interact to create balance and stability: the somatosensory system, the visual system, and the vestibular system.

Information that comes from the joints, muscles, and receptors such as the muscle spindles and golgi tendon organs is *somatosensory*. This information travels through different parts of the brain, relaying information such as joint positions and facilitating agonist and antagonist muscle contractions to help the body maintain balance and stability.

The *visual* system adjusts the input that comes in from both the somatosensory and vestibular systems. *Vestibular* receptors detect linear acceleration changes in postural alignments, and differences in angular velocity from movements of your head. This is the master control system that makes the final decision on how to balance the body when all information is in.

Flexibility and strength may also help determine the balance and overall stability of the body. Insufficient range of motion and being too weak to balance and stabilize yourself in certain drills or game situations may cause problems. The flexibility and strength program detailed in chapters 6 and 7, if done properly, should help you excel when it comes to body control on the court.

Balance and stability work has been built into your resistance training program to save you time and also to help you work on stability when dealing with outside forces. For example, performing single-leg dumbbell presses and other single-leg movements while standing will help challenge your balance systems.

I have also included some basic balance training skills that will give you a good idea of how your body responds when faced with different situations and body positions that can create instability.

Shoes can help add support and give you more contact surface area with the floor, thereby helping you maintain proper balance. Thus, I recommend that you perform these drills with your shoes off to help create more instability.

Single-Leg Balance

Stand on one leg with your hands on your hips or across your chest and hold your balance for 30 to 45 seconds without touching your opposite leg to the floor. While standing on the one leg, bend your other leg so that the upper part of that leg is parallel with the floor. To make this drill a little more challenging, close your eyes and move your head up and down or from side to side.

Relevé Position

Stand on one leg and hold your position while in a plantar flexed position (on your toes). Dancers and gymnasts call this a relevé position. This can be very difficult because of the small base of support. Try to maintain your balance for 15 seconds or more. Perform this exercise with your eyes closed to make it more challenging.

The ankle is very unstable in a plantar flexed position, so training the ankle in this position can improve overall stability in this particular joint. To help maintain balance in this position and over this small support surface, keep your ankle stiff during this exercise.

Single-Leg Three-Point Floor Touch

While standing on one leg, squat down and touch the floor in front of you and return to your starting position. Next, squat down and touch the floor to the right of you; then return to your starting position and repeat the drill by squatting down and touching the floor to your left. During your squat on one leg, keep your chest up as high as possible. Try to bend at the knee joint instead of at the waist.

To make the drill more challenging, arrange any type of small balls (such as golf balls) in a triangular pattern on the floor. Place the first ball one to two feet out in front of you. Place the second ball one to two feet to the right, and place the third ball to the left at the same distance. This adds a visual concept to the drill. Do not look directly at the balls when you pick them up. Use your peripheral vision. Remember to keep your chest up when squatting down. Perform the drill for 45 to 60 seconds on each leg.

T Balance

Sometimes you must keep your balance and control on the basketball court despite being in an awkward or unusual position. You're not always able to maintain an upright position during play. Start this exercise by standing on one leg with your hands on your hips. Bend your upper body so it is parallel with the floor. Point your down foot and your upper body in the same direction. Hold your opposite leg up and straight, parallel to the floor, with your body forming the letter T. Stay in this position 30 to 45 seconds; then switch legs. To make the drill more challenging, while you are in the T position, try rotating slightly (three to four degrees) from side to side without falling.

Single-Leg Short Hop

While jumping and landing on one leg, do a series of short hops while trying to maintain balance and control. When landing, try not to double hop, and make sure you come down on the ball of your foot and not on your heel. Go 15 to 20 yards on one leg, then go back with the other. To make the drill more challenging, have your coach or partner throw a five- to eight-pound medicine ball to you when you land (at chest level), then throw it back using a chest pass just before you jump.

Single-Leg Bounding and Balance Triple Jump

Start by standing on one side of the sideline or baseline on one leg. You will perform three consecutive jumps on one leg as far as possible down the line. Let's say you start on your right leg (on the right side of the line) and jump out as far as possible to land on the left side of the line, then immediately jump out as far as possible and land on the right side of the line, then once again bound out as far as possible and land on the left side of the line. At the end of the final jump, stick the landing and hold it for at least two seconds. This drill is great for single-leg explosiveness and balance. See how far you can bound and still maintain balance when landing after the last jump.

Swiss Ball Balance Work

In this exercise, use a Swiss ball that is soft and mushy. Put both knees on the ball, keeping your upper body upright while squeezing and keeping your abdominal area tight. Try to stay up, without falling, as long as possible. Make sure that you are in an open area so that if you do fall, you do not get hurt on any hard object. To make this exercise even more challenging, have your coach or partner slowly toss a three- to eight-pound medicine ball to you at chest level. Repeat the movement with a medicine toss back to your partner, all without falling.

Single-Leg Resistance Work

As I pointed out earlier, some of your balance work is written up in your year-round resistance training program. Single-leg dumbbell presses, side raises, squats, and medicine ball work are just a few that you can do to make your balancing work more fun and challenging. I also suggest performing balance work with free weights while standing on a pad, such as an Airex pad or some thick foam rubber. Anything that adds to the instability of your movement is great for making your body strive for balance in the face of different outside forces. Be creative in all aspects of your balancing work!

Ball Handling and Dribbling

Although dribbling is a very important part of your game, it can be misused or overused. You have to learn when to dribble and when not to dribble, even if you are a point guard. If you dribble too much, your teammates will tend not to move, which can make the defense's job much easier. Too much dribbling can hurt teamwork and morale.

Dribbling is a touch skill, not a sight skill, so you should learn to dribble up the court without watching the ball. You can achieve this by focusing on the offensive goal while dribbling and looking over the entire court using your peripheral vision. Control the ball with your fingers and the pads of your hand, not the heel of your hand. Spread your fingers comfortably and cup them around the ball.

Also learn to dribble with both hands. When your are being heavily guarded by a defender, it helps to know how to protect the ball with your opposite hand and your body, keeping the ball low and to the side of your body. Always dribble with a purpose; know where you are going and what you are doing.

I have included several ball-handling drills in your workouts to be inserted whenever time allows. Remember that the more time you practice dribbling, the better ball handler you will become.

Tennis Ball Dribble

With a tennis ball in each hand, dribble the length of the court and back. Do not catch and throw the balls down but actually dribble both balls at the same time or alternate your dribbles. You may even want to work on your crossover dribbling or your spin moves with a single tennis ball when you feel comfortable doing so.

Basketball and Tennis Ball Dribble

While dribbling a basketball with one hand, throw a tennis ball to your coach or partner with the other. Your partner then throws the tennis ball back for a total of 5 to 10 throws. After you have completed the throws, switch hands. Work on improving your coordination with both your dominant and nondominant hand.

Crossover Dribble

A crossover, or switch dribble, is a basic move that you can use in the open court only when there is sufficient room between you (the dribbler) and the defender. In this drill, you push the ball quickly and keep it low across your body. Proper technique is to push the ball from left to right (or vice versa) while performing a zigzag move from left to right. During game play, make this move before the defender gets too close.

Between-the-Legs Dribble

This dribble is used to avoid overplay by a defender and to change the ball from one hand to the other. When doing this dribble, keep the ball low and cross it between the legs with a quick and hard push. To help with the coordination of the dribble and the footwork, walk forward down the court slowly while crossing the ball over between the legs every step.

Backjack

Start by standing at one end of the baseline. On the coach's command, start dribbling toward center court. Every time the coach blows the whistle, stop your forward movement and begin dribbling backward. Your coach should command several changes in direction before you finish at the opposite baseline. To make the drill more challenging, on the whistle, demonstrate various skills such as dribbling behind your back or even between your legs.

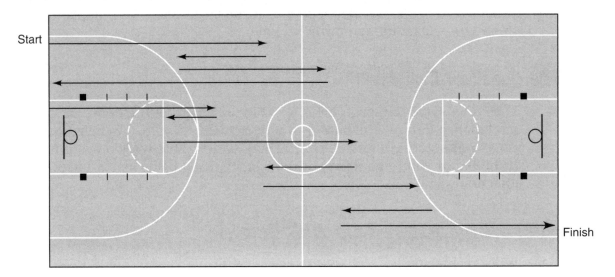

Bleachers

Begin by dribbling the ball at the bottom of the bleachers. On the coach's command, start dribbling the ball up the bleachers slowly, keeping it under control. Do the following:

1. Use your right hand only.
2. Use your left hand only.
3. Alternate the ball between hands.
4. Move freely up and down the bleachers without stopping.

For safety reasons, do not race up the bleachers during this drill.

Finger Count

The objective of this drill is to develop dribbling skills without looking at the ball. Start by facing a coach who is standing at the top of the three-point arch. The coach starts backing up, reversing direction, and zigzagging. The coach also at any time holds up one hand and raises and lowers a different number of fingers. Follow or mirror every movement the coach makes while dribbling the ball. Every time the coach holds up a certain number of fingers, shout out the number. Go slowly at first; then, when you get the feel of the drill, pick up the pace.

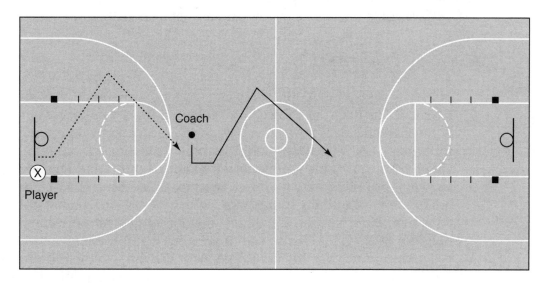

Midas Touch

This drill is great for improving hand-eye coordination and focus.

1. While continuously dribbling from a standing position, slowly and carefully sit down on the court, dribble there for 10 seconds, and then return to a standing position while still dribbling.
2. While sitting on the court with your legs spread, dribble the ball around your body two to three times; then repeat in the opposite direction.
3. Place one knee on the court and lift the other knee up. Dribble the ball around your body under your up leg.
4. In a standing position, dribble the ball back and forth behind your back 10 to 15 times. The ball must remain behind your back during the entire drill.

Lights Out

While dribbling up and down the court slowly, have your coach or partner turn the lights on and off in the gym. If turning the lights on and off is a problem, use a blindfold to ensure that you have no visual contact with the ball. Focus on your hand making contact with the ball.

Two-Ball Dribble

While dribbling two balls around the gym, do the following:

1. Force the balls to hit the court at the same time.
2. Force the balls to hit the court at different times.
3. Dribble the balls so that one ball has more contact with the court than the other.
4. Dribble one ball low and the other high; then switch.
5. Dribble both balls as low and as fast as possible.

Obstacle Course

This drill is great for conditioning and learning to maintain a strong dribble when fatigued. The diagram shows how to line up the cones for this course. Starting at the baseline, dribble with your right hand to cone 1. At cone 1, lie down and do 10 push-ups with both hands. Dribble with your left hand to cone 2 and do 25 full sit-ups. Dribble with your left hand to cone 3 and balance on your right leg while dribbling with your left hand for 30 seconds. Dribble with your right hand to cone 4 and do 10 push-ups with a ball under each hand. Dribble with your right hand to cone 5, balance on your left leg, and dribble with your right hand for 30 seconds. Dribble with your left hand to cone 6 and jump rope for 100 jumps. After your 100 jumps, go in for a layup, get the rebound, and dribble quickly down to the opposite end of the court for a jump shot at the elbow. Shoot 10 free throws and repeat the drill.

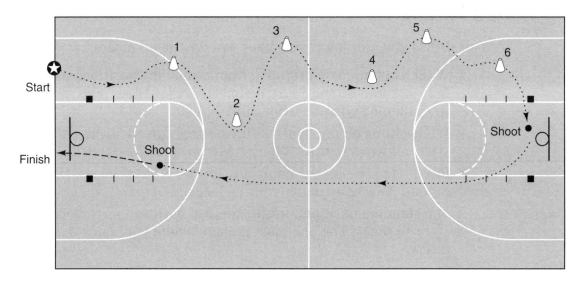

For More Information

Appleton, Brad. 2002. Stretching and flexibility. www.bradapp.net/docs/rec/ stretching.

Brittenham, Greg. 1996. *Complete conditioning for basketball.* Champaign, IL: Human Kinetics. (Greg is the strength and conditioning coach for the NBA New York Knicks.)

Brzycki, Matt, and Shaun Brown. 1993. *Conditioning for basketball.* Chicago: McGraw Hill/Contemporary. (Shaun is the strength and conditioning coach for the NBA Boston Celtics.)

Cohen, S., and A. McLaine. 2002. The implementation of balance training in a gymnast's conditioning program. *Strength and Conditioning Journal* 24 (2): 60-65.

Goldberg, Lorne, and Peter Twist. 2001. *Strength ball training.* Champaign, IL: Human Kinetics.

Grabow, Mark. 1996. *The on-court 100.* Lafayette, CA: Pro Fit Training Systems. (To order, call Grabow at 510-986-2269. I highly recommend this book for good drills. Mark is the strength coach for the NBA Golden State Warriors.)

Gummerson, Tony. 1990. *Mobility training for martial arts.* London: A&C Black.

National Basketball Conditioning Coaches Association. 1997. *NBA power conditioning.* Champaign, IL: Human Kinetics. (This book was written by many of the top NBA strength and conditioning coaches.)

Marandino, Roger. 2002. Shared power. *Pure Power Journal* 2 (March) (2): 60-61.

O'Bryant, Harold, and Mike Stone. 1986. *Weight training: A scientific approach.* Edina, MN: Burgess International.

About the Author

Chip Sigmon is the athletic trainer for the Carolinas Sports Performance Center at Carolinas Medical Center. He was the strength and conditioning coach for the WNBA's Charlotte Sting, and he served the Charlotte Hornets as their strength and conditioning coach from 1994 to 2001 prior to their departure to New Orleans.

Sigmon has worked with such notable athletes as Alonzo Mourning, Baron Davis, Hersey Hawkins, Andrea Stinson, and Dawn Staley. As an assistant strength coach at the University of North Carolina (1982 to 1983), he worked with Tar Heel and NBA greats Michael Jordan and Brad Daugherty. He was the head strength coach at Appalachian State University from 1984 to 1989.

A graduate of Appalachian State University, Sigmon is a former competitive body builder and an NSCA-certified personal trainer and fitness consultant. He has written articles for a national basketball newsletter and for the NSCA, and he was a contributing author to *NBA Power Conditioning*. Sigmon is also a sought-after motivational speaker and is on the State Speakers list for the Fellowship of Christian Athletes.

When not busy training athletes, speaking at conventions, or writing, Sigmon enjoys working in the yard, reading, and spending time with his wife, Michelle, and their two daughters at their home in Charlotte, North Carolina.